AN EMBARRASSMENT OF CRITCH'S

AN EMBARRASSMENT
OF CRITCH'S

Immature Stories from
My Grown-Up Life

MARK CRITCH

VIKING

VIKING

an imprint of Penguin Canada, a division of Penguin Random House Canada Limited

Canada • USA • UK • Ireland • Australia • New Zealand • India • South Africa • China

First published 2021

www.penguinrandomhouse.ca

Library and Archives Canada Cataloguing in Publication

Title: An embarrassment of Critch's : immature stories from my grown-up life / Mark Critch.
Names: Critch, Mark, author.
Identifiers: Canadiana (print) 20200404598 | Canadiana (ebook) 20200404679 |
    ISBN 9780735235090 (hardcover) | ISBN 9780735235106 (EPUB)
Subjects: LCSH: Critch, Mark. | LCSH: Television actors and actresses—Canada—Biography. |
    LCSH: Motion picture actors and actresses—Canada—Biography. | LCSH:
    Comedians—Canada—Biography. | LCSH: Newfoundland and Labrador—Biography. |
    LCGFT: Autobiographies.
Classification: LCC PN2308.C75 A3 2021 | DDC 791.4502/8092—dc23

Book design by Leah Springate
Cover design by Leah Springate and Terri Nimmo
Cover images by *This Hour Has 22 Minutes* © 2021. Photo from *This Hour Has 22 Minutes* used with permission from 22M Holding Company Inc. under exclusive license by 22M Hour Productions (NS) 29 Inc. All Rights Reserved.

Interior images courtesy of the author unless otherwise specified. All photos from *This Hour Has 22 Minutes* used with permission from 22M Holding Company Inc. under exclusive license by 22M Hour Productions (NS) 29 Inc. All Rights Reserved.

Printed in Canada

10 9 8 7 6 5 4 3 2 1

Penguin
Random House
VIKING CANADA

For Melissa. Thank you for taking me home.

PROLOGUE

If you read my first book, *Son of a Critch*, you will know that I was born and raised in Newfoundland and Labrador. That book told the story of my childhood and where I got my sense of humour. This is the story of my adulthood and what I did with that sense of humour.

I'm writing this book from Gower Street, in St. John's. It is arguably the oldest city in North America. I say "arguably" because it is not but we love to tell people that it is. If I left my house and lay on my side I could roll myself straight into the Atlantic Ocean. I have almost accidentally done that on many late-night walks home from the pub.

The people of my province have always been known for their wit. We have offered up more than our fair share of comedians to the national stage. Maybe there is something in the water, besides salt.

I recently discovered that the most famous joke in the world was born a stone's throw from my house. In 1899, a Canadian snake oil salesman named Doc Kelley visited St. John's with his travelling medicine show. Kelley would travel to far-flung places and entertain crowds who may never have seen a show before. Kelley's shows were meant to gather punters to which he would sell bottles of his Shamrock Oil, which he claimed was good for "headaches, earaches, toothaches, neuralgia, cuts, scalds, sprains, rheumatic aches and pains." Kelley would sell his "medicine" for fifty cents a bottle, then leave town before anyone noticed that the medicine was probably better used as a disinfectant.

The self-styled doctor was trying to raise a crowd for his performance one night when he found himself watching a show of a different kind. A cook was arguing with his kitchen boy and the yelling had drawn a small crowd. The cook threw a half-eaten piece of pie at the boy, hitting him in the face. The crowd of onlookers burst into laughter, giving Kelley an idea for an experiment.

He bought a pumpkin pie, staged a fight with his banjo player and at the exact right moment, he slammed the pie right into his partner's face. The audience of Newfoundlanders erupted into laughter. No one had ever seen anything so funny before, Kelley incorporated the "pie in the face" into his act, and slapstick comedy was born. Kelley's bit was stolen and used by Charlie Chaplin, Buster Keaton, Bugs Bunny and millions more all over the world.

Pieing, as it's now known, works best when the person being pied is of higher status than the person throwing the pie. Charlie Chaplin always pied the cop, not the other way around. That's why activists often pie politicians. A protestor pied former prime minister Jean Chrétien in 2000. "I'm not that hungry," he quipped.

Like Doc Kelley, I have travelled the world trying to entertain people and, like him, I have never laughed harder than I have in my hometown of St. John's. I don't pie prime ministers but I have made fun of several to their face and the effect is pretty much the same. This book is the story of my travels and the siren call that brought me home again.

Unlike Doc, I believe laughter is the best medicine. I hope this book will cure what ails you.

1

LEAVING HOME

———————————

"What do you want to do when you grow up?" my father asked me. I was taken aback. I was seventeen at the time. I thought I *was* a grown-up. I was too young to know I wasn't an adult—old enough not to know better, but young enough not to know a damn thing. Ignorance is bliss and I was the happiest man on earth.

My father, on the other hand, was seventy-six. He was a retiree with a high school graduate on his hands. I was what my Catholic family would call a "blessing" but what most people would acknowledge as an accident, or at the very least the result of one too many beers at the office Christmas party. I was the hangover that just wouldn't go away.

I suppose Dad looked at my graduation day the way a warden might look at his last remaining prisoner's parole date. A certain amount of freedom was on the horizon for both parties involved. "You could get a trade," he suggested. We both knew that wasn't an option. I was a thin, asthmatic epileptic with weak ankles. I couldn't see myself taking a welding course any time soon. This conversation had been coming and we had both avoided it like a married couple pretending they hadn't already been divorced for years. The admission was simply a formality.

"I want to be an actor," I said, aging my already grey-haired father another decade he couldn't afford to lose. Dad avoided my hopeful gaze. He looked down at his brown leather dress shoes. They were scuffed from years of work and worn into something comfortable yet still formal, much like he was.

"I could get you a job researching deeds," he said, deflecting my truth like Wonder Woman blocking a bullet with her metal bracelets. My father came from a time when you took a job because you could get one, not because you chose it. His father had died of tuberculosis when my father was just five years old. His mother went "in service," scrubbing the floors of wealthy St. John's families while my dad roamed Water Street for odd jobs to help keep a roof over their heads. He would remind me that he had fought "tooth and nail" to crawl out of the grip of poverty. Now, I was trying to shake its hand.

He'd known this day was coming, though. There had been plenty of warning signs. I had been in school plays. I'd formed a sketch comedy troupe. I spent every free moment writing. My room was filled with scripts and costumes. There was no escaping it. His son was an artist. "I want to be an actor," I argued. "It's who I am."

"But you could still be yourself on the side, couldn't you?" he countered. "Good god. This is not the time to be clowning around with that foolishness. The arse is out of 'er."

The only job my father had left in life was to get me on a steady path, and his method was somewhere between a bird gently nudging its hatchling out of the nest and a man tossing a bag of garbage onto the curb without looking to see where it may fall. But he had a point. I was entering the job market just as thirty-five thousand other Newfoundlanders were put out of work overnight.

When John Cabot first "discovered" my homeland of Newfoundland in 1497 (much to the surprise of the native Beothuks who lived there), he wrote that you merely had to place a basket over the side of the ship and when you pulled it back up again it would be teeming with cod. You didn't even need a net.

By the time I graduated from high school in 1992, though, you couldn't find a cod if you drained the ocean. Decades of overfishing had depleted the cod stocks. In a desperate move, the federal minister of fisheries and oceans, John Crosbie, a Newfoundlander himself, shut

4

down the northern cod fishery after five hundred years, ending the greatest fishery in the world with the swipe of a pen.

Crosbie was labelled a traitor. When a group of angry fishermen surrounded him on a wharf, he stood tall and told them that *he* "didn't take the fish out of the goddamn water." If it hadn't been true, they might have killed him. The moratorium was meant to give the species time to rebuild but they still haven't come back. Maybe, like many other Newfoundlanders, the cod had simply moved to Alberta to work in the oil sands. Nobody knows.

I had wanted to become an actor in a part of Canada where, months earlier, it was much more realistic to become a fisherman. But in 1992 that situation changed, and my chances of making it as a comedian were suddenly just as feasible as a life at sea. There was no future in either.

None of the sudden economic disaster affected my family, though. My father was a newsman. He worked in AM radio, and bad news was good news for the Critches. I grew up right next door to his radio station in the capital city of St. John's. My bedroom view was of satellite dishes and radio towers, not waves and lighthouses.

I didn't know any fishermen. I hadn't even been outside of the city in my life. The Critches were not nomadic people. I would watch in wide-eyed wonder as the richest kids in my class showed me the pictures of their family vacations. Florida! New York! Moncton! Our family never went anywhere. We only took one trip a year and it was not to Disneyland or MarineLand. It was to Newfoundland.

We would pack our bags and take the bus to the park that lay eight kilometres away. The old man acted as if that eleven-minute drive was akin to Lindbergh's hop across the Atlantic. A lunch was packed, watches were synchronized, and the night before was a restless one.

"Mary," my father would shout to my mother, having shot upright in his bed, "do you have the bus schedule? When's the last bus? Good god! We don't want to miss that! We'll be stranded. We'll have to sleep on the street."

Nobody enjoyed the trip to the park more than my father, and he hated it. Dad never changed out of his suit. He would watch me splashing in the pool like he was paying by the water drop. "Isn't that long enough?" he would ask, staring at his watch. "You're plenty wet now." He wouldn't calm down until we were sitting on the bench at the bus stop, a full three hours early. I'd stare out the window on the ride home, dripping onto the faded vinyl seat. I was fascinated by the strange neighbourhoods that whizzed past me. I wished that I could spend some time exploring that world. I wanted that almost as much as I wished I had been allowed to change out of my wet trunks before we boarded the bus.

Once home, I'd sit on the front step of our house and watch the cars as they headed out of town on the highway. I'd have gladly climbed into any one of them just to say I had been "somewhere."

Newfoundland was the only place in the world that I had ever been and even that was a mystery to me. There are two types of Newfoundlanders: townies and baymen. My people were townies, but I was bay-curious.

Townies don't come from a town at all. They come from a city—the capital city of St. John's, to be precise. Baymen come from the rural outport communities of the island. The term is not gender-specific. Women, children, thems and theys can all be baymen.

A bayman might think of a townie as being soft and too stuck up to talk to, whereas a townie might think of a bayman as being uneducated and rough. As with most stereotypes, there are outright lies in these descriptions. And as with most lies, there is some truth to them, too. Despite their animosity, in 1992 there was one thing that both the baymen and the townies could agree on: nobody wanted the fishery to end.

The government of the day came up with a program called the Atlantic Groundfish Strategy, or TAGS for short. Under it, people could extend their unemployment insurance benefits while they trained for jobs outside of the fishery. The problem was, as my father kept reminding me, there weren't any jobs outside of the fishery. The towns where these people lived had been founded on one thing and one thing only—fish. It would be harder still to find many people who were willing to go back to school in their fifties after dropping out of school as teenagers to work in the fishery. But the government was desperate to get people back to work, no matter how ridiculous the scheme.

Some women decided to retrain as hairdressers, practising on their friends and families. Their customers looked at their terrible haircuts and thought, *I could do better than that.* And so they, too, retrained to be hairstylists. Soon the bays were full of hairdressers chasing each other up and down the road with curling irons. Hair was bleached, curled, flat-ironed, coloured, braided, extended, woven and teased until it fell off the head in an apparent act of hair suicide. I believe the technical term is "barbicide"—or that might be the blue liquid that stylists clean their combs in. I did not retrain as a hairdresser and am therefore not an expert.

There have been lots of crazy ideas floated to try to save the New-foundland economy—a hydroponic cucumber farm, a rubber-boot factory whose managers were alleged to be German Nazis on the run and a hydro project that is currently more than $6 billion over budget, to name a few. And I soon found myself a job as part of one of the craziest.

Rising Tide Theatre, in Trinity, about a three-hour drive from St. John's, produced locally written shows about the Newfoundland and Labrador experience. Donna Butt was and still is the company's artistic director. She is a force of nature wilder than any North Atlantic gale. She writes, performs and produces original work in a place where, before her, it was almost unheard of. Donna is like the flower that grows up from the middle of the sidewalk: it makes no sense that she exists, but there she is. Like many Newfoundlanders, she is able to make ends meet through a mix of passion for where she lives, drive and being too stubborn to know better.

Donna, along with playwright and actor Rick Boland, created a project that would use TAGS money to retrain the recently unem-ployed to be actors. Now, to retrain an unemployed person to be an actor is basically just retraining an unemployed person to be more unemployed, but I wasn't about to argue because, as an actor, I was unemployed. I was offered a part in their summer theatre festival and

I jumped at the chance, both to advance my career and to prove my father wrong.

"I got a job," I told my father.

"Thank god," he said, breathing out a sigh that filled the room with Rothmans smoke. "You spoke to Andy Richards about that job researching deeds?" My father's life had become so routine that even a life researching a deed seemed glamorous.

"No. It's an acting job," I said.

"Is that smart?" he asked, expertly coughing out and inhaling smoke at the same time. "In this economy?"

"I only got the job because the economy is bad," I explained. "If the economy was good there wouldn't be no money in getting us out of the bad economy. Poverty is a growth industry, Dad."

"Hang on to Andy Richards's number," my father advised.

There was a catch. Taking the job would mean that I would have to leave my beloved "town" and move to "the Bay." I'd be working in the town of Trinity, population 169. My new job was a three-hour drive from home. This would be the farthest I had travelled in my life. I was about to make Neil Armstrong look like an agoraphobic.

I did not have a car, nor much of anything, at the time. So I bought a ticket on the shuttle service that connected St. John's to the various small towns and outport communities known, affectionately, as the Bay Bus.

The meeting place for this one-car caravan was a small office across the street from a church that had now been transformed into a strip club. The pole replaced the altar and the lap-dance stalls now stood where the confessionals once were and prayers of a less godly type were now answered. The sad jingle-jangle of a small bell announced me as I opened the door to the office to find the place empty except for a lone dispatcher who sat, his back to the room, yelling into the receiver of a rotary-dial phone.

"For frig sakes," he bellowed, the cigarette smoke shooting from his nostrils like dry ice at a Mötley Crüe concert. "I'll get there when I friggin' gets there! Frig off!" Slamming the receiver down, he lit a fresh cigarette from the dying embers of the one in his mouth. He let the stub of his last smoke fall from his lips, like a bullet casing being ejected from a machine gun, hot from hours of battle. His lower lip instinctively reached for the new one, ready to reload.

"When's the next bus to Trinity?" I asked, hearing the hesitation in my voice.

"Trinity?" He stood up, and as he did, stacks of brochures and bills slid off his desk to join the piles of ash on the floor, daring a fire to break out. "I think I know where that is."

"I think I know where that is" is not something you want to hear your bus driver say.

The phone rang again and he shot it a look as if it had just said something bad about his mother. "Come on," he said, and reached back to grab a set of keys from his desk that looked like they belonged to the jailkeeper at the Tower of London. "You're in luck. The Bay Bus is leaving right now."

I followed him and hopped aboard the van, taking a seat in the back.

"What am I? Your chauffeur, am I?" he asked. *Well, yes*, I thought. *Yes, you are.*

"I just got one stop to make," he said, starting the engine with a sound that can only be described as a death rattle. Despite being a warm spring day, he cranked the heat, and soon the combination of heat and smoke made me feel like I was being barbecued alive. He pulled up to a row of townhouses. They would not be filming any tourism ads on this street; a Crime Stoppers PSA, maybe. "I'll be right back," he said. "Keep her running."

I felt like a child left outside a store to ride up and down on a mechanical pony. What would I do when my quarter ran out or the van exploded? My only comfort was that this drive couldn't get much worse. Then the townhouse door was flung open and my wayfaring driver emerged, carrying a large suitcase and an infant's car seat.

A woman appeared on the step with a baby on her hip. She must have had very strong hips because this baby was huge. The child looked to be under a year old but had enough flesh to stretch out and cover a

9

forty-year-old man. It looked like it had been weaned on KD sauce and gravy. Maybe he'd be more comfortable driving?

"Who the frig is *he*?" the mother bellowed, pointing directly at me.

"Customer," my driver shouted back.

"You never said nothing about no customer! I'm not stopping every five minutes for him to pee. My mother is expecting us," she howled as I began to suspect that these two had met before. The ancient baby stared at me and I was not man enough to stare back. The mother had brought plenty of Huggies, but it seemed more like a job for Depends to me. The creature on her hip grabbed a bag of Cheezies from his mother, like an alligator pulling a newborn fawn into a muddy river.

I opened the door and moved to the passenger seat. "I'll let you get in back with your, uh, little one," I stammered. I didn't want to admit that I was afraid the baby might bully me.

"Oh? I'm a bad mother, am I?" she asked. "Arsehole," she muttered as she reluctantly climbed into the back with the Churchillian child and slammed the door. The now familiar sketchy-carnival-ride sounds of the van resumed and we were finally on our way. I took my script from my bag and began to study my lines.

"Too good to talk to us, are ya?" the driver alleged.

"Pardon?" I asked, pretending not to have heard.

"What do ya want to go reading a dumb old book for?" he asked.

"It's not a book. It's a play," I clarified, immediately regretting it.

"A play?" He laughed. "Hear that? Alistair Cooke here is reading a play!" He began to laugh again and was soon joined by his whatever-she-was and eventually even the Bay-baby was laughing at me. The driver's laughter soon turned to a wet cough and he rolled down his window to spit into the road. The slight breeze offered relief from the heat and the pungent diaper air for a moment and I breathed in as much as I could.

"What's the name of it?" he asked, lighting a cigarette from the dashboard lighter.

"*Salt-Water Moon.*"

"*Salt-Water Moon. Salt-Water Moon.*" He spoke the words aloud, trying them out. He had never said those two words together before and spoke them as if he was tasting a new recipe for the first time and was trying to decide if the ingredients complemented each other. "What's it, like, a space movie, is it?"

"No," I replied, "it's a love story. About a guy trying to win back his girlfriend."

"What did he do to her?" my fellow passenger asked. "The buddy. How come the girl left him? Did he cheat on her with her cousin?" What a strangely specific guess. "Maybe somebody saw him and told her!"

"Yeah?" the driver volleyed back. "Maybe whoever told her was a friggin' liar who should mind her own business."

None of that was correct. I explained that *Salt-Water Moon* was written by an ex-pat Newfoundlander named David French. "It takes place on a moonlit night in 1926. Mary Snow is waiting for her fiancé to come visit her but her old boyfriend, that's me, surprises her. My character left her behind to head up to Toronto to make his fortune. But since he heard she was engaged, he comes back to win her heart."

"I woulda killed him," the baby's mother said. "He only came back cuz he was jealous of the other fella. She breaks off that engagement then he'll just take off on her again. Leave her there all alone with the baby."

"There isn't a baby in the play," I corrected her. The child glared at me like a dog that knows you're talking about it but doesn't know if what you're saying is good or bad.

"Maybe he just needed some time," the driver argued. "Like, maybe he felt trapped and needed some space. Like, he's only young, right? Buddy just probably needed to sow his oats is all and now he's ready to man up. Right?"

"What about *her* needs?" the mother asked. "She doesn't get to sow her oats, does she? She got a baby to look after!"

"There's no baby," I reminded them.

"You know your part?" the driver asked, changing the topic before he became it.

"Pretty much," I answered, surprised that he was taking such an interest in the arts. He pulled the script from my hands.

"Okay, then. Let's do it. I'll be Mary."

We hurtled down the Trans-Canada Highway at 120 kilometres an hour as our driver thumbed through the pages of my script to find his lines. "Okay. Go!"

At least it would pass the time, I told myself.

"'Hello, Mary,'" I began. "'Aren't you even going to acknowledge me? The least you could do is make a fist.'"

The driver sped up slightly as he read. "'It—was—you—I heard.'" He was horribly miscast.

"'Some welcome home this is,'" I emoted.

"'What—did you—expect?'" He struggled to find his character's voice, drive and smoke all at the same time. "'Why, it's the Prodigal Son, boys! All the way back home from Toronto! Strike up the drum!'"

"That's it, girl," the audience chirped from the back seat. "Tell him to try minding the baby for a night and see how he likes it!"

"'There's no call to be sarcastic,'" I said, gaining confidence in my performance. "'It doesn't become you,'" I cooed. "'A yellow dress becomes you, Mary, more than sarcasm.'" And with that we were off. I, as Jacob Mercer, charmed my Mary, a forty-something deadbeat-dad bus driver, and won his hand. Our audience was split. One half truly identified with this tale of lost love redeemed. The other half threw up some Cheezies, crapped himself and fell asleep. Tough room. But if I could act here, in this van, I figured, I could act anywhere.

"This is you, townie," the driver said, breaking me from the self-admiration necessary for a career in the arts. "Trinity!"

I grabbed my bag from the back and stretched as I took in my new home. A small gas station stood on a ribbon of road with a few houses scattered along the nearby hills that gently rolled down to the ocean. A sign read "Port Rexton." The van began to pull away.

"Hey, wait!" I called after it. "This isn't Trinity!"

"You're close enough," the driver said as he started rolling up his window. "Trinity is just through Port Rexton and across the water.

Can't miss it. Call me if you get stuck for a Mary." Then, with two fast barmps of the horn, he pulled away. I'm pretty sure that the baby gave me the finger.

I hadn't been a bayman for more than a minute and I was already lost. I had left the city for the first time in my life, and for the first time I was homesick. You can take the townie out of the town, but you can't take the town from the townie.

2

TRINITY

I WAS SURROUNDED BY ETHEREAL beauty. The sun was setting. Icebergs stood majestically on the other side of a lighthouse. People go their whole lives hoping to experience that kind of natural beauty one day. But it was all lost on me because I was lost. Night was coming on. It was getting cold, I was tired and I really needed to pee.

I started walking. The road seemed endless. I walked longer than I had ever walked in my twenty years of life. I must have been walking for nearly fifteen minutes.

I dragged my plastic carry-on suitcase behind me. Its wheels locked up as small pieces of gravel from the side of the road became jammed in the casings. It was like a stubborn child in a supermarket that refused to move another inch until it got a candy.

An old pickup truck slowed down alongside me to match the pace I was walking. The driver peered at me from behind transition lenses. He was wearing a flashy cowboy shirt, the kind of shiny shirt that singing cowboys wore at the Grand Ole Opry. If the true-crime books I'd read had taught me anything at all, it was that I was about to die.

He leaned over the passenger/victim seat and rolled down his window. "You da townie?" he quickly mumbled.

I nodded. He pushed open the door and returned his gaze to the road. With no other options, I wearily picked up my albatross of a bag and hopped in.

"Thanks for the lift," I said. The ice did not break. The chill in the air caused the ice to thicken until it rivalled the iceberg out in the bay. "I'm Mark," I offered.

"Yup," he said with a nod. Occasionally as we drove he would point out something he thought would be of interest, but he spoke too quickly for me to understand. He spoke as if he expected you to already know what he was going to say before he said it and mouthing the words was just some sort of formality.

"Now that over there's a mumberly-humble-hambel. That there is the gumble-gamble but you can't mumber-gash the tummer-lum or you'll end up in the gunny-ford."

I'd nod and feign interest as if I had just been shown the booth where Lincoln was assassinated. "Oh, you don't say. Isn't that something!" Here and there I would catch a word or two that I recognized, but they never seemed to go together.

"Over there is the canny-coop CRADLE. Tummle-docker inda CEMETERY. You can fundle-pop the trundle conna CODFISH. Tunny-alla-gust up in the SAND."

We crested a hill and I was silenced by the panoramic view of sea and land that met my eyes. When you first see the town of Trinity, your mouth drops open at its timeless beauty. Brightly coloured houses, many dating from the 1800s, dot the landscape. Two wooden churches dominate the skyline, towering over narrow paths lined with white picket fences. All of this is surrounded by water as if the ocean itself was hugging the town to protect it and keep it as its own ancient secret.

Trinity was settled in the mid-sixteenth century, and you get the feeling that a ghost from that time would not feel out of place if it was wandering those same streets today.

We passed a forge. "Grumble-mumble Blacksmith," my guide exclaimed, having long since been inured to the effects of the view. A sign claimed the shop had been in operation since 1795.

"Dandle-duddle-other Blacksmith," he said, pointing to another forge across the street from the first one. This must be downtown Trinity, I figured. I had never lived in a town with two blacksmiths before. No matter what happened, at least I would be sorted for nails.

"Dis is da spot dey gotsya put," he said, and pulled up to the house I would be staying in. A long row of rickety steps led to a small bungalow that hung off the side of a hill overlooking the ocean. It perched precariously over the bay on stilts that made it resemble a daddy longlegs. The house clung to the cliff as if it was threatening to jump. Its paint was peeling in places to reveal a hundred years' worth of colours layered over each other like a folded quilt. It looked as if it had seen better days, but in a town this old, I imagined pretty much everything had.

My new home lay straight across from a lighthouse. The fog had started to creep its way across the bay and the foghorn began to blast, almost as if it was warning me to go back home.

"Fubba-gonda fixer-upper," my driver said as he began to pull away.

"Wait!" I shouted, calling after the closest thing I had to a friend for miles. "What's your name?"

He squeezed the brakes and looked perplexed. "Jim," he said, and shook his head as if I had just asked him what my own name was. Like *Cheers*, I was clearly living in a place where everyone was expected to know your name. I regretted my suspicions of Jim. He was not the serial killer I'd feared he was. He was just a friendly man who wanted to see me settled. I was the stranger here and it was up to me to fit in, not the other way around. Jim was not speaking too quickly. I was listening too slowly.

I watched the lights of his truck disappear over the ridge and with that, I was alone.

I lay in my bedroom that night as the mournful wail of the foghorn filled my ears. The beam from the lighthouse would sweep my room with every rotation as if I was trying to sleep in the courtyard of Alcatraz during a prison escape. This was one hell of a nightlight. I worried that the spindly legs under my home would give way, tossing the house and its contents, including me, into the ocean. I couldn't swim, but I knew I wouldn't die a coward's death, crying to be saved. Thanks to the foghorn, no one would ever hear me. I would drown alone, in total darkness, then blinding light, then total darkness, then bright light, darkness, bright light, darkness . . .

Suddenly I heard the screech of tires, a foghorn, footsteps, a foghorn and then a fist pounding at my door. I jumped from my bed, worried that the knocking would send my little house into the hungry sea.

I flicked the light and opened the door to find three sets of eyes staring at me. One man was tall and slender, one short and stocky, and the third was a brawny fellow who had a tattoo of an anchor on his arm. *I can't believe this*, I thought. *I'm actually being visited by Popeye.* I was the only one of us without a moustache.

"You the townie?" Popeye asked.

"I guess I am," I said, unsure if this was a social visit or a home invasion. "I'm new here. I mean, I'm Jim's friend."

"We're in the play with ya," the little one said.

"But we're from here," said the big guy. My new co-workers looked me up and down. They weighed my worth with their eyes but the needles on their mental scales didn't seem to move an inch. I was six feet tall and weighed in at 130 pounds of bone and bushy hair with oversized round glasses. I was the cliché of a townie.

I was new in town and, being such, I was a thing to be stared at, like a new exhibit at a zoo. I expected a sign would be placed on my door: "Do not feed the Eastern Spineless White-Breasted Townie."

"You're coming with us," the little one said. "We're going for a drive." As with Jim before them, I immediately feared the worst of my co-workers. I might never become a famous actor, I figured, but at least I would end up as a character on an episode of *Dateline*. I squeezed into the back of the tiny speedster. It felt like I was trying on a coat that was two sizes too small. My knees touched my earlobes. For some reason the big one with the tattoo was in the back with me. He passed me a beer as we shot down the winding road of the village like Secretariat escaping a glue factory.

The two in the front watched me through the rear-view mirror in anticipation. I was being tested. I took a sip of beer and smiled. The two in the front exchanged an approving glance and the big one beside me cursed under his breath. Someone had lost a bet. We took a curve in a hurry and he slid towards me, pinning me against the door.

"You like music?" the driver asked. Yes, I loved music. Having older parents, my tastes leaned more on the side of Frank Sinatra and Perry Como. I doubted these fellows were into "Strangers in the Night" or "In the Misty Moonlight," though both were appropriate. "Pick a tape," he said as his co-pilot passed me a case of cassettes.

One look at the contents and my suspicions were proved right. I was being tested. There were only three tapes. One was by the eighties Canadian band Glass Tiger. This was standard radio fare of the time. Next to it was an AC/DC cassette. You can play fiddles and accordions all you want, but if you really want to captivate Newfoundlanders, play "You Shook Me All Night Long." The letters "AC/DC" had been written on more faded jean jackets there than "Levi's." I looked at the last cassette. It was 1987's eponymous chart topper from teen-queen Tiffany. This was a trap. Picking it would prove I was a useless townie. This was overkill. I was playing Russian roulette with a gun loaded with two blanks and one armour-piercing bullet.

My hand paused for a moment over her cassette for dramatic effect and then I swiftly selected the AC/DC tape. "Play 'Shook Me' for me," I said, smiling smugly. All three of my captors nodded at each other. The secret ceremony of the beer and tape finished, I was accepted into the group. The skinny fella was Rod. The shorter man, Doug. And the guy with the tattoo was Dennis. None of them was very excited about acting, but times as they were, they had no choice. Dennis was hoping to get up to the mainland to work on the lake boats. Doug was thinking about giving it all up and becoming a plumber. Rodney thought he might go up north and give carpentry a shot. But they all had families they couldn't bear to leave. To me, this acting was a dream job. To them it was mere survival.

A dirt road lay among the bushes and trees and we took it at high speed like Batman driving into the Batcave. Huge clouds of dust surrounded us as the road became an old railroad bed that Doug knew by heart. This was dangerous, for sure, but would I have been any safer in my bed, hanging off the cliff like an egg in a seagull's nest?

"This is smoke alley," Doug told me, as the dust from our tires obscured both our licence plate and the driver's vision. Dennis hit "eject" and soon Tiffany blasted from the tape deck. "I think we're alone now! There doesn't seem to be anyone around!" Truer words were never spoken.

~

The main attraction of Rising Tide's theatre festival was the Trinity Pageant. The actors would lead their audience along the pathways of the town and recreate historic moments with dramatic tableaux. Many of them had once worked in the fishery they now performed, donning historically accurate costumes to portray gainfully employed versions of their current selves. They had, in effect, become their own ghosts.

As audiences roamed through the town, the cast would run ahead of them and lie in wait. I played one of the pirates who sailed along Trinity's coast in the early seventeenth century. I was, perhaps, the least intimidating pirate to ever walk that rocky coastline.

Throughout the afternoon, tourists would hear from a recent widow of one of the twenty-four men in the tiny community who froze to death while hunting seals in 1892. They would watch as the first small-pox vaccine in North America was administered. And in a haunting scene, they would fill a mercantile shop as the merchant told the fishermen that their fish was not worth the cost of the supplies used to catch it. This would mean a slow starvation over the long winter for the fishermen and their families. You know, some light-hearted fare for the tourists.

As the weeks went on, the crowds grew into the hundreds. You could tell who was from Ontario by how they dressed. We weren't the only ones in costume. If someone had a Tilley hat, rain gear, a walking stick, a travel wallet, a backpack and pants with more pockets than stitches, they were a mainlander. Tourists would outfit for an African safari just to take in a two-hour play in a place with sidewalks.

This was a lot of added foot traffic for a town of just 169 residents, and not everyone was happy. One of the locals took to choosing the same time each show to start up his chainsaw. As an actress struggled to be heard by the people at the back of the ever-growing crowd, this man and his chainsaw would drown her out in a protest of sorts.

Ed Kielly was our stage manager. He was like a tornado in pants. Long grey hair flowed behind him as he rushed to and fro, kept alive by a mix of nitroglycerin pills for his heart, coffee and an unrivalled passion for theatre. Ed cocked his head to the buzz of the chainsaw. "Come on, young fella," he said. I followed, still dressed like a pirate, into the little corner store across from the blacksmith's. Ed headed for the cooler and emerged with a case of beer. "Nudding in the world that a case of beer won't fix," he said. This may have been the most useful lesson I have ever learned.

The unhappy local saw us coming and he lifted his chainsaw. I waved my arms like a messenger begging a soldier not to shoot. Ed hoisted the case of beer over the fence with a clink. "Every time you don't start that chainsaw, I'll give you a half-case. Deal?" The local weighed self-satisfaction with self-lubrication and gave an unconvinced but definite nod. I had my first lesson in how to assimilate into a culture. Be respectful, and bring a half-case.

For a time, the chainsaw's owner would stand there holding it in his hands at the start of each show, threatening to cut the silence in two until he got his ransom, but as the weeks passed, I'd find the chainsaw just sitting on the stump. Its owner, tired of the drama over drama, learned to trust us. Each show, Ed would pass the case of beer over the fence and carry on without even stopping.

As the audiences grew and more tourists came, the challenge was to come up with new experiences for them to enjoy. We travelled to the abandoned community of Ireland's Eye to put on a show about resettlement. In the 1950s the Smallwood government came up with a centralization program to move people from the small outports to larger communities, where it would be cheaper to provide government services. Before Confederation, Ireland's Eye had a population of 157. Now the place was a ghost town, and the church spire tilted as if bowing to the forsaken souls in the graveyard. It made for an eerie location.

"We should bring in a weed whacker," Rod said as we wandered through the brush. "Clear out the cemetery. Nobody here got anybody to tend their graves anymore. It's not right." And so we did. We pushed through the trees until we came to a graveyard where the grass nearly kissed the tops of the tombstones. We cut it back and said a silent prayer. I wondered how many communities in the province were in danger of succumbing to a similar fate without the fishery. How many people would die wondering if there would be anybody left to tend to their graves?

I had felt like a fish out of water when I first arrived in Trinity. Helpless, I flipped and flopped on the wharf, gasping for air and struggling to survive. I was only a three-hour drive from home but I might as well have been in Tokyo. I didn't speak the language. But I began to pick up a few words the more I listened. I was even beginning to understand Jim. But I was still as much of a tourist as the people who came to see our shows. I vowed to earn my place.

Without a proper theatre, we were forced to be creative. We performed a show about ghosts in a graveyard. We did a play about the railway on an abandoned train car. Our audience, watching from their cars, would beep their approval. We debuted a play by Kent Stetson about the 1914 sealing disaster, in which seventy-seven men died on the ice. The concrete foundation of an abandoned whaling station was painted to resemble an ice floe. It was easy to convince yourself that you were lost at sea with the ocean lapping at the beach behind you and the brisk evening air in your lungs. Kent Stetson's *Harps of God* went on to win the Governor General's Award for Drama in 2001.

The grand experiment was working beyond anybody's wildest expectations. Word spread, and directors from Toronto and the Stratford Festival wanted in. With each season, more and more actors came from town to join us. But by then, the locals were as experienced as any big-city performer. What they had, you couldn't teach. They were natural storytellers and they were as much of the place as the trees and the water. You can't fake that.

~

The ever-growing audience meant we were always in need of more shows to give them. Donna Butt decided that our next show would be *A Midsummer Night's Dream*. Shakespeare! I was excited. This would be a chance for a guy to act! But that night at Rocky's, the boys looked glum. "I don't know about this," Rod said, picking the label from a bottle of beer. "Shakespeare. I can't learn that. Ye crowd are nuts!"

"That's just it," I said, pouncing on the opportunity. "You're already speaking Shakespeare! You just said ye!" I flipped through my script in a frenzy. I borrowed a pen from Rocky behind the bar, circled a word and tossed the script down on the table. "Ye! Read that!"

Rod lifted the pages and, squinting in the darkness of the bar, began to read. "'Ye spotted snakes with double tongue . . .'"

"See?" I said. "Shakespeare is full of Newfoundland words. This place was settled when Shakespeare was still writing. His accent was preserved here. People make fun of the way we talk but we're the only ones still speaking Shakespearean English. It's the mainlanders that talk wrong, not us!"

One day, after rehearsal, we saw a new sign on the beach advertising sea kayak rentals. This was just another in the string of businesses that had come to Trinity in the wake of the Rising Tide. "Never been *kicking* before," Doug said, crumpling the word up in his mouth as if it was a bill he was refusing to pay. "I says we goes for a spin." Dennis and Rod gave a holler and ran towards the kayaks like sailors on a desert island who had just spotted a passing ship.

I followed behind, reluctantly. I couldn't swim. I had nearly drowned twice and still remembered the sharp sting of water being pumped from my lungs. I had no problem with boats, but bobbing across the Atlantic Ocean in a little plastic tube seemed suicidal to me.

"You have to know how to roll the kayak," the instructor told us as my testicles rolled up into my lower body cavity. "You'll need to hip-snap your kayak upright and into the recovery position."

"Go 'way, b'y," Dennis said as he started to bounce around the ground in his kayak. "It's the Atlantic Ocean. You'd be dead by then."

Comforting. I could not envision a single possible outcome that didn't end with a Coast Guard helicopter fishing my corpse out of the water. The only thing that gave me the courage to go was my even greater fear of looking like a townie in front of the boys.

We paddled through the safety of the harbour and out onto the open ocean. There is a moment that comes when you realize that you're actually in the Atlantic. The waves begin to rise and fall as if they are the pulse of the planet itself. I closed my eyes, matching breath to the waves I rolled on. In. Out. Up. Down.

"You all right, buddy?" I heard Rod ask me.

"I'm great," I lied. "Never better. So much fun." In. Out. Up. Down.

I'm not sure if I felt the spray upon my face or heard the sound first. The sound was unlike anything I had ever heard before but I immediately knew what it was. I opened my eyes to see a humpback whale gliding past us, the mist from its blow covering me in a baptism of sorts.

"What the frig do we do now?" Dennis asked, but nobody answered. There was nothing to say. All we could do was bob up and down like corks in the ocean and hope we didn't get in its way. I could see the white underbelly of the beast as it swam upside down beneath us, the pale flesh appearing bright green in the water. Decades' worth of scars and barnacles decorated its elegant body.

I had never seen a whale before, even though my great-grandfather had been a whaler. He drowned in 1856, and after his death his son abandoned the hard life of the cruel sea and made his move into town. He died in St. John's of TB when my dad was five. And fate made me a townie.

The whale made one more pass and it seemed to look right at us as it did so. Was he staring at me and thinking, *Wasn't your great-grandfather the prick that killed my great-uncle Finnegan?* It raised its mighty tail to signify a deep dive, or maybe to flip us off, and disappeared into the depths.

Our close encounter finished, I paddled back to the small beach and crawled towards dry land. I lay on my back on pebbles smoothed by centuries of waves lapping away their rough edges. If I stayed here long enough, I wondered, would the waves wear me down, too?

That night, the audience walked a path along the shoreline to our fairy garden. We performed *A Midsummer Night's Dream* under the stars by torchlight. This troupe had formed to keep people employed long enough for them to qualify for EI. Now twenty thousand people a year were coming to see them perform Shakespeare. The whole experience in Trinity had been a midsummer night's dream of sorts, and whenever I made the long drive into town, I felt like I was leaving home, not driving back towards it.

Against all odds, the little bungalow on the cliff had become a haven to me. I remember dancing on the roof of the place on a star-filled night while my friend Des Walsh sat in a kitchen chair alongside me playing his fiddle. There was no foghorn that night, just "Auntie Mary" swirling through the salt-sea air, punctuated by the occasional sound of a whale breaching in the distance. For the first time in my life, these were the sounds of home.

~

In 1997, my third summer in Trinity, Her Majesty the Queen came to Newfoundland. To commemorate the five-hundredth anniversary of John Cabot's landfall in Newfoundland, a replica of his ship, the *Matthew*, sailed from Bristol, England, to nearby Bonavista. Betty Windsor and her husband, Phil, were just two more tourists to our part of the world that year, so like we did whenever tourists came, we performed for them. Donna was tasked with putting together a performance that would recreate Cabot's "discovery" of the New Founde Land, or what the native Beothuk people would call "the day the neighbourhood went to hell."

We had started in the streets of a town of 169 people. We had performed in fields. We had performed in graveyards. And now we were going to perform in front of the world. Before I came to Trinity, I had wanted to see the world. Now, it felt like because of Trinity, the world had come to me.

The Queen was to arrive as the *Matthew* sailed round the bend and the crowd of thousands cheered. The event was emceed by the Newfoundland pope, actor Gordon Pinsent. Gordon was the star of countless films and TV shows, an author, director and playwright and was easily the most recognizable person from our province. The crowd was as happy to see him as they were to see Her Majesty, if not more so.

The event was broadcast live around the world. Peter Mansbridge, the anchor of CBC's *The National*, provided commentary to all of the folks across Canada. Like it does whenever important events happen in Newfoundland and Labrador, it rained. We went live. A cannon fired. The *Matthew* came into sight. The crowd erupted into cheers. But there was no Queen.

MANSBRIDGE: The royal motorcade is stuck in that traffic jam we saw out there in that highway we saw coming into town.

The Queen was stuck in traffic. No one had ever been stuck in traffic in Newfoundland before. Occasionally, traffic slowed down to let a moose cross the road but even then it only ever stopped if the car hit the moose. The people went from cheering to applauding to soaking wet to silent.

Eventually, the fanfare played and she emerged from her car like Punxsutawney Phil on Groundhog Day. I wanted to make sure it was her. I pulled a twenty-dollar bill from my pocket. It was the old twenty with the portrait of a young Elizabeth on it. I balled it up in my hand to wrinkle the paper and age the portrait, then spread it flat again. Bingo! It was her!

Our then premier, Brian Tobin, ended up splashed all over tabloids in the UK for a major faux pas. He touched the Queen's lower back, arguably in what we would call the "arse area," to help her up the stairs. You are not supposed to help the Queen of England up stairs by pushing her by her arse like a cow up a truck ramp, apparently.

MANSBRIDGE: See those chairs? They were short some chairs. They needed special chairs for the royal party so they came to our hotel last night and whisked them all out of the lobby area.

They covered the Queen in a thick blanket, but I wasn't sure if the blanket was to keep the Queen warm or to protect the fancy stolen lobby chairs from the rain.

MANSBRIDGE: It is chilly, as we said. Minus four degrees Celsius with the wind chill in the Bonavista area today.

I had never pitied a queen before but I sure did that day. Soaking wet, freezing and about to sit through a show that even we knew was not that good. I played one of Cabot's crew. Of course, Cabot hadn't "discovered" anything at all. The Beothuk people were already living here. There are no Beothuk people living today because the people who "discovered" them killed them all. My character's lines came directly from a letter written about the landfall to the Lord Grand Admiral of Castile.

"'We disembarked and in that particular spot, we found a trail that led inland.'" I bellowed against the rain. "'We saw a site where a fire had been made and a stick, half a yard long, pierced at both ends and painted with brazil.'" I had no idea what brazil was but I said it like I had been painting sticks with brazil my whole life. "'By such signs, we believed the land to be inhabited.'" Here I was, at an international celebration, spouting concrete historical evidence that this "discovery" was really more of an invasion. My royal performance was complete, and I waited for the reviews to roll in.

MANSBRIDGE: It is *very* cold here, ladies and gentlemen, and they were in those little costumes. Some of them were having a real hard time trying to stay warm. It is cold, minus four here. And it's taken its toll on a lot of people. Some members of the crowd have filtered off. It's too cold and windy for them.

So I guess you could say that they were "blown away"? Good. All that was left was for the Queen to come meet us. She shook Gordon Pinsent's hand, no doubt telling him how much she liked Babar. She greeted the captain of the modern-day *Matthew* and his crew and congratulated them on a job well done. She took flowers from the little girls who had been step-dancing in their summer dresses on a day that would have made Peary turn back from the pole.

With each person she greeted, she seemed to speed up a little as the stiff Newfoundland breeze pelted hail against the one side of her face I knew so well from the quarter. Short conversations became handshakes. Handshakes became nods. Nods became glances. Then she looked right at me. I could see there was some math being done behind the royal visage. She had the look on her face of someone who, having asked for a menu, decided they didn't want dessert after all. It was time to go.

She met my gaze again as she drove past me. I was sure I could hear the door lock. I still taste the bittersweet disappointment of this day every time I lick a stamp. I would not meet royalty again until I hosted the Miss Teen Newfoundland contest in 1999.

That was my last year working in Trinity. I had learned a lot about acting but even more about myself. I learned more about Newfoundland and Labrador in those few summers than I would in the sum total of the rest of my life. The fish never did come back. But the tourists did, year after year. The Trinity Pageant still plays today to tens of thousands of people each year. For me, though, like the Queen after a play in the rain, it was time to move on.

I had wanted to be an actor. And I was making a living as one. But these were not the bright lights of Broadway that I had pictured myself in as a child. I had dreamt of big-city excitement, but I had been afraid to leave the nest. Trinity had seemed like the end of the world to me, but now I could see that it was just the start. Plus, the long stretches of unemployment between summers as an actor were starting to become too erratic. I needed consistency. I was going to become a full-time comedian. I was going to aim for total unemployment.

3

PAYING DUES AND
BOUNCING CHEQUES

N 1997, WHEN I DECIDED that I would leave Trinity behind and try to make it as a comic, I joined the cast of Rising Tide Theatre's annual satirical sketch show. It featured a look back at local headlines that lampooned the politicians of the day. It was also where I first learned to turn a headline into a sketch.

But I was no stranger to sketch comedy. I first performed original comedy in 1990, when I was fifteen years old. I was not an athletic child. I couldn't catch anything that didn't lead to a lung infection. In high school, I fell in with the theatre nerds and, in doing so, I found my people.

I, like all cool, red-blooded young men, signed up for a clowning workshop. I was partnered with a tall, skinny boy named Stephen. We both wore glasses. His hair, like mine, was a mushroom cloud of unkempt curls that showed neither of us was deep enough into puberty to worry about our looks. Stephen bragged that he was a juggler, and that comforted me. I had found the only person in the tenth grade who was a bigger nerd than I was.

We were drawn to each other like two antelope in the Serengeti who sensed that the formation of a herd might lessen their chances of being eaten. "Do you want to start a comedy troupe?" he asked me, breaking the only rule of our mime workshop.

We found two other guys to join our troupe and struck a deal with a local theatre to let us perform for a split of the door. We performed a three-night run in a cabaret slot at eleven on school nights. None of our friends could come but luckily a few drunken Russian sailors from the boats tied up in the harbour wandered in. Alcohol makes for a forgiving audience.

I can still remember the hypnotic rush of standing on that stage at the age of fifteen and getting that first big laugh. Just days before, I had been sitting on my bed, plucking words seemingly from mid-air. I had written them down and memorized them, repeating them to myself like sacred prayers. Now, in the spotlight, they had returned to me as laughter—and the occasional groan. How on earth could I ever do anything else again?

Acting felt important, but sketch comedy felt right. I've always preferred it to doing stand-up. It's the difference between being a solo artist and a band. What's the point of playing if there's nobody to play with?

In 1997, I found myself back doing what I loved most. We would play St. John's and then hit the road, travelling to every nook and cranny of the province. Some nights we would take a ferry to a small community to perform. Audience members would drag cafeteria chairs onto a basketball court while I would crank up the basketball net that hung over the stage in the town's gymnatorium.

When the show was over, we would boot it back to the wharf to catch the last ferry and drive through the night to reach our next gig. I had once sat on the front stoop of my parents' house and wondered where the highway went. Now I knew its turns as intimately as the workmen who painted the lines on it. I couldn't believe my luck.

But when the tour wrapped, I found myself unemployed again. To make ends meet, I took a role in a dramatic production that toured high schools. The point of 1990s children's theatre was not so much to entertain kids as to terrify them. There were only three possible topics for shows then: teen pregnancy, drug addiction or STDs. I was cast as an HIV-positive high school student in *Fear of the Young*. My character contracted AIDS, was shunned by his friends and disowned by his parents, and at the end of the show he commits suicide. It was hardly the feel-good hit of the year.

Occasionally, we were joined by a young woman who was HIV-positive. She would speak to the kids after the show about living with the disease. A picture of the performance made the front page of the local paper. The photo showed me standing in front of a group of young people, emoting my heart out. The headline read "Youth with AIDS Speaks to School."

My phone rang early that morning. It was my father. "Good god!" he shouted down the line from a payphone next to his favourite newsstand. "I have to find out that you have AIDS in the paper?"

"Read the caption," I said and waited.

"Oh," he said, and hung up the phone. This was the closest my father and I ever came to having "the talk."

To finish the run, we had been booked to perform at a correctional facility for young offenders. The kids were brought into a small multipurpose room where we performed just inches away from our captive audience. The show was as far away from comedy as I could get, but you would never know that by the amount of giggling in the room. One of the kids in the front row leaned in, tapped me on the knee and said, "Hey, buddy! You're giving me heartburn." This was followed by the biggest laugh I've ever been onstage for.

The lights flicked on and a heavyset guard puffed his way to the front. "Okay, Tyler," he barked, "that's it! I told you if you don't listen while the man here tells you about his AIDS, then you're going to get taken out."

"I don't really have it," I murmured. "It's just a play."

"Tell the man you're sorry," the guard said, taking the boy's arm.

"Sorry you got AIDS, buddy," the kid said, rolling his eyes.

"I'm acting," I murmured as the boy was pulled up through the audience to chants of "Ty-ler! Ty-ler! Ty-ler!"

I'd never been so excited for my offstage suicide. Each show, I would place a roll of cap gun ammo on a brick and hit it with a hammer to simulate a gunshot. In the darkness of the wings, I kept missing. Klang-klang-klang-klang. The audience chatted amongst themselves as I pounded away like a blind blacksmith. Eventually I just shouted a half-hearted "bang," returned to the stage for a bow, and walked back offstage, dejected and defeated.

A few months later, my friend Tristy Clark and I were walking towards Signal Hill, which overlooks St. John's Harbour. I hadn't worked since the touring show and there was absolutely nothing on the horizon. I was not just the-phone-bill-will-have-to-wait-until-next-month broke. I was I'll-have-to-wait-until-I-find-an-ATM-that-gives-out-fives broke.

A giant anchor at the base of Signal Hill marks the entrance to the Battery, a small fishing community where brightly coloured houses cling to the cliffs above the harbour like nesting puffins. As we approached, the anchor was swarming with about a dozen young people. Boys were shoving each other to impress the girls who could not be less impressed. They spotted us as we tried to scurry past and the kids were soon snapping at our heels like small dogs chasing a car.

"You guys are looking to buy condoms, are ya?" a young man said as he swaggered towards us. He must have been about eighteen years old, though his wispy moustache and problem acne made him look much younger. This ragtag group of lost boys and girls seemed to answer the unasked question, What if Peter Pan sold weed?

"Hit the one with the glasses," a girl said in far too casual a tone. The entire group looked back to her, somewhat shocked by the sudden acceleration from insults to assault. It was as if she had used the wrong fork at a fancy dinner, betraying her upbringing. Like the boys trying to court her, she was moving way too fast.

"We're both wearing glasses," Tristy said as I slipped mine into my coat pocket.

The oldest boy appeared keen on the girl and he charged at me like a moose in heat to impress his cubic zirconia in the rough. I was about to be rolled by the Little Rascals.

"Wait!" a boy called from the back. "I knows him. This fella came to do a show for us when I was in the boys' home." It was the heckler Tyler. I was glad to see that the rehabilitation had worked and he was now on the straight and narrow, jumping hikers with his friends like stagecoach bandits. He nodded, and the bigger boy released me. "Leave them alone. He's all right."

Then he turned back to me and lowered his voice. "How you feeling these days, buddy? With the you-know-what. Any better?"

There was no point in explaining. "Much better now, thanks," I said. He gave me a wink as if to say my secret was safe with him. Tristy and I made our way up the hill. The streetlights were just turning on and the city reminded me of a Christmas tree. I couldn't help but smile. Yes, I had almost been beaten up by a group of children. But I had also just been recognized as an actor for the first time in my life. Things were looking up.

~

I met Sherrie Winsor when she was dating one of the members of my comedy troupe. She was outgoing, funny and beautiful. She lit up any room she was in and was a lot of fun to be around. So much fun that the second they broke up, I made my move.

Sherrie worked in a photo lab in St. John's. For those younger readers, a photo lab was a place where people took something called film to be developed. You know the ten seconds between taking a picture on your phone and uploading it to Instagram? That used to take a week. If you wanted to look at a stranger's vacation pics in the nineties, you had to stand by the window of the photo shop and watch as the freshly developed pictures fell from the printer and onto a conveyor belt to dry. "Oh look," you'd say. "They were in Disneyland. Fun! Oh no! Their grandmother died. Such lovely flowers. Oh! Somebody had a birthday!"

Things between Sherrie and myself were going well—when we found ourselves in the same town, that is. In the pre-FaceTime world of the nineties, being on the road in Labrador meant I may as well have been working in Cairo. I was often out on the road, either acting in short runs of plays or building up my stand-up act by accepting gigs that I didn't have enough material to fill. And so my relationship with Sherrie had devolved into a litany of lost letters and missed telephone calls.

I didn't have a cellphone. I didn't even have the money to pay hotel phone bills. Most "romantic" calls went like this.

Ring
SHERRIE: Hello?
AUTOMATED VOICE: You have a collect phone call from . . .
ME: Hey, Sherrie! It's Mark! I'm in Gander at a payphone! The show went great! I'm going to Grand Falls tomorrow! I really miss your—
Boop!
AUTOMATED VOICE: Please deposit twenty-five cents.

Some of the hotels I stayed in didn't even have phones in the rooms. You'd have to go to the front desk and ask if there had been any calls.

ME: Excuse me. Any messages for Critch in room 208?
DESK CLERK: Uh . . . yeah. Some girl called. Says it's "urgent."
ME: What girl? Was her name Sherrie?
DESK CLERK: Don't know. I only wrote down "urgent."

On that particular day, I had to use the desk phone to call back while the desk clerk hung on every word as if she was watching *Days of Our Lives*.

ME: Hi. Just got your message. Sorry. I just got in. When? I think I'm back next Monday. I miss you!
DESK CLERK: What a sin.
ME: The show went great. We had a good crowd and—
DESK CLERK: Show? You in a band? Or are you a hypnotist?
ME: Do you mind? What? No, not you, Sherrie! I was talking to someone else. No! I *am* listening!

DESK CLERK: Bet you can't hypnotize me. Give it a shot. Read my mind.

ME: That's not what a— Leave me alone! No, Sherrie, not you! Can it wait until I'm back? Hello?

Boooooooooooop.

ME: I think I ran out of time on my calling card.

DESK CLERK: You're running out of time, all right. You need to stop talking so much and listen to what your girlfriend has to say. Some hypnotist you are. Can't read *her* mind, can ya?

When my gig was over, I rushed back to town as fast as I could. "What is it you wanted to talk about?" I asked Sherrie.

There was a pregnant pause before she told me she was pregnant. With life, as with comedy, timing is everything. I was about to become a father and I was unemployed.

Sherrie and I moved into an old row house and did our best to make it a home. Months passed, and I was still making close to nothing. Thanks to Sherrie's job at the photo lab, we had been slowly acquiring all the things you needed for a baby. We found a cheap used crib and a brand-new Diaper Genie. We were almost ready for parenthood. All that was missing was a baby and a job for me to help feed it with.

~

Finally the phone rang. If I wanted, I could play a "corporate." Such gigs are much coveted among performers. Conferences, office parties, conventions and the like pay good money for the privilege of ignoring a performer while everyone gets drunk and networks. A blue-collar company up north wanted me to play their Christmas party. They'd fly me up, take care of my accommodations, and all I'd have to do was forty minutes of comedy after their dinner. I was going to make five hundred bucks. I was going to be rich.

I boarded the nineteen-passenger twin-engine plane and buckled up. At times, we almost seemed to be flying backwards as we pushed deeper into a harsh winter storm. We landed the way a lawn mower would land if you threw it off the roof. I grabbed my bag and looked around the empty airport for a sign of life.

A man entered the hangar through the automatic doors and brought the harsh winter wind in with him. "You the comedian?" he asked. "I guess you heard what happened?"

"I didn't," I replied.

"Best if the boss tells you," he said. "We're going to his house now, anyway. Your room isn't ready yet." We pulled up to the house and went inside. The porch was filled with more boots than I had ever seen in one place in my life. Clearly, I wasn't the only houseguest. A woman I assumed to be Mrs. Boss came out of the kitchen holding a casserole.

"You the comedian?" she asked. I nodded. "Here," she said, passing me the dish. "I don't see what's so damn funny, though," she muttered, just loud enough for me to hear.

Cigarette smoke hung in the air as the men sat in silence around a table playing cards. The Boss spoke to me without looking up from his hand.

"You the comedian?" he asked. I was beginning to sense a pattern. "You better be damn funny. One of our guys died today."

"W-what happened?" I sputtered. I shouldn't have even asked. The wound was too fresh to be discussed with a stranger holding a casserole.

"They found him hanging from the ceiling of the meeting room," he explained. Everyone winced at the image.

The man who'd picked me up from the airport raised a fork and began to eat from the casserole dish I was holding. He spoke to me in between bites.

"Your room is attached to the meeting room," he told me. "Room's off limits. They brought in a grief counsellor to talk to people."

"Wait," I said. "They're holding grief counselling in the room where the guy killed himself?"

"Where else would they have it?" the Boss asked. "The meeting room is *for* meetings."

The phone rang and my driver picked it up, thankfully cutting the conversation short.

"Hello. Okay. I'll send the comedian over. Yeah. I don't know either. None of this is very funny." He hung up the phone, turned to me and continued eating. "They're all done over there. There won't be anywhere to get food this hour of the night so you better take that casserole with you," he said, his hefty gut pushing the dish up against my stomach. "Make sure you bring the dish back."

"Spacious Rooms and Luxurious Suites" promised a sign in the window of my accommodations. My driver and I passed several lovely rooms without stopping until we came to two large doors that most certainly did not open onto a Jacuzzi suite with premium cable. "This is you," he informed me guiltily. He opened the door onto a large meeting room where six orange plastic chairs were arranged in a semi-circle. My eye was drawn to the drop ceiling above them. One tile was missing, and a support beam had bent slightly from the weight of something. I wondered what that could have been.

I paused, uncertain if I should even enter the room. It seemed disrespectful, and besides, I didn't want to leave any fingerprints.

"You're in here," he said, flipping a switch and entering what I can only describe as a storage closet with a kettle in it. A small desk was built into one wall. A single window filled the other. A cot lined the remaining wall. "The crapper is in the other room," he said, finishing the tour.

Someone had thoughtfully placed two dozen bottles of beer at the foot of my bed. I was only going to be there for two nights. If they expected me to drink twenty-four beers between now and showtime, it was going to be one heck of a performance.

He opened the desk drawer to reveal a pornographic magazine. "There's a skin mag here for ya, if you gets lonely," he said with a wink. *Oui Hot 'n' Horny* was the title of the publication. I wondered if I could fall asleep standing up.

"See you in the morning," he said, nonchalantly walking under "the spot" on his way out.

"Wait!" I shouted after him. "What happens in the morning?"

"Snowmobile run," he informed me. "We'll come get ya around seven. Enjoy." He looked at the open drawer and wagged his finger at me as if to scold me for being a naughty boy. He hit the switch on the way out of the meeting room, which also plunged my room into darkness. I tried my best not to scream.

I closed my eyes and, what seemed like moments later, I opened them again to the roar of a dozen snowmobiles and a fist pounding on my door. My friend was back, dressed exactly the same but wearing a helmet. "You didn't touch your beer," he said. "Too busy reading, were ya?"

As we thundered off down the road, I held tight to the rear handgrips. We formed a long convoy of machines, travelling from house to house, shed to shed, for a couple of drinks as if we were Santa Claus drinking milk and cookies.

The conversation was always the same.

"They going ahead with the dinner tonight?"

"They should cancel this. It isn't right."

"You better be some frigging funny."

By the sixth shed, I was wobbly with drink and it was barely noon. They eventually dropped me back at the hotel and I quickly changed into my suit. Any sensible person would cancel, but I had a kid on the way and I was too afraid to go back to my room.

I stood looking out at the banquet hall. A hundred couples were enthusiastically eating stuffed chicken dinners but the mood was dour. I felt a tap on my shoulder and turned to see a man in a suit.

"I'm the emcee. Just so you know, a few people here tonight said they don't think it's right to have a comedy show, so you may see some couples getting up to leave when you start. Don't take it personally. Ready?"

I thanked him for the pep talk.

"There's just one other speaker and then you're up, okay?" He walked up to the podium and tapped a butter knife against a wine glass. "I'd like to thank the Ladies' Auxiliary for the lovely meal," he began. "I know a lot of people said we should cancel the dinner tonight. But the room was already booked for next weekend, so here we are. Anyway, we have a very special person who has something to say before I bring out our guest speaker." Then he introduced the widow of the man who had just died.

A hush fell over the crowd as she walked to the podium.

"I came here tonight because I know a lot of you thought about cancelling," she began with a quiver in her voice, "but I want you to know that he always loved these dinners and he would have wanted it to go on. I do, too. Just remember the good times because—" She began to cry.

The audience burst into applause. The reaction was unlike anything I had ever seen. The ovation must have lasted two full minutes until she whispered her thanks and left the stage.

"Your next speaker," the emcee said, "is Mark Critch. He's a comedian. I'm sure he'll do fine. Mark?" This was followed by the kind of silence an astronaut would hear if they removed their helmet in the darkness of space in the seconds before their head exploded. As we approached one another on the stage, he paused briefly and whispered, "If you get stuck, there's an old guy named Joe here. He has a really old truck. That might be funny." Then he walked right past me, washing his hands of the whole thing, like a priest having given a death-row convict the last rites.

"Thanks for that warm introduction," I began. The crowd looked at me as if I was a defendant at the Nuremburg trials. "What a meal. Got to love Newfoundland and Labrador food, right? Newfoundland cookbook: kill it, boil it until the colour drains out, add gravy and serve. Bon appétit! Am I right?"

"I thought it was lovely," someone in the back muttered.

"Yes, of course," I said. "Just lovely." A couple in the back stood up and walked out. Other tables were beginning to chat amongst themselves. They hungrily eyed the door, deciding if they should join the other deserters before dessert came. They had seen enough death that weekend. They didn't need to watch me die onstage, too.

I looked to the emcee, hoping he would put an end to this misery. He smiled and mimed driving a car with his hands. Why not? It wasn't like things could get any worse.

"Is there a Joe here?" I heard myself ask. An older man in the back of the room raised his hand. He was wearing a ball cap and the kind of suit a man buys intending to eventually be buried in it.

"Wow, Joe," I said. "You look even older than—your truck." Silence. Everyone looked back at old Joe and waited for a response. I felt like I was watching a kettle boil. His shoulders started to jiggle, he smiled, and then he took off his hat and slapped it on his knee as he laughed. The next table joined in and I watched as the laughter moved around the room like an aftershock with Old Joe at the epicentre.

"I hear Joe parked his truck in front of the museum and it got towed—inside the museum!" Huge laugh! Boom! "I don't want to say Joe's truck is old, but I hear he drives an F-50!" Zing! "Joe doubled the value of his truck. He filled it up with gas!" Some gentle ribbing of an old man and his truck seemed to be just what they needed to take their minds off their troubles for a bit. I went back into my act and finished to a huge round of applause.

Everyone wanted to buy me a drink. The Boss shook my hand and told me that he was so impressed that he was going to drop off a hindquarter of caribou to my room. I'd never been tipped with wild game before.

Old Joe came over and gave me a hug. "Buddy, you have to take a ride in my truck. You're after making it famous now." I could use a ride. I had a hindquarter of caribou to pack. We climbed in with Joe's wife.

"What did you think of that meal?" he asked. "Wasn't that something?" I confessed that I hadn't eaten anything because of my nerves, and Joe immediately turned the truck around. "You didn't eat? You're coming home with us and I'll cook you something."

The lights of the hotel faded in the distance as we pulled into Joe's driveway and made our way inside. Their cozy house was filled with the flotsam and jetsam of a life well lived. Joe turned on the TV, the way many older folks do for background noise. His wife went and sat silently facing me, her back to the television, neither interested in it nor in me.

Joe made his way into the kitchen and I could hear pots and pans clatter as he searched for just the right tools to prepare a feast. "How's about a fried bologna sandwich on toast. Mustard OK?"

Mrs. Joe settled into her recliner, her eyes quickly shutting after the big night out. My attention shifted from her to the TV behind her. The commercial ended and the announcer said, "We now return to *Fridays Without Borders* on Showcase." My heart stopped dead in my chest. Showcase was a Canadian TV channel that showed soft-core porn films after eleven p.m. These were the kind of movies teenaged boys snuck out of their bedrooms to watch. It was low-budget cable featuring French-Canadian movies wherein subtitles translated words like "Ooooh" and "Ahhh."

The screen flickered to reveal two women kissing as a man watched through an open window. They began to undress as one of the women kissed her way down the torso of the other. Joe entered the room with two toasted bologna sandwiches on a tray, unaware that he was about to discover his wife and a stranger watching French-Canadian erotica in his own living room.

He placed his culinary masterpiece down on a tray table with a flourish. "There ya go, buddy. Dig in!" He glanced towards the television and saw what can only be described as a three-headed human sex pretzel.

"What the hell do you have on, missus?" he shouted. She woke and looked at the TV just as both women knelt to undo the man's belt. She shot me an accusatory look as if I had snuck into their house to watch porn while she was sleeping. Old Joe grabbed the clicker and tried to change the channel but only succeeded in making it louder. "Ooohs" and "ahhs" filled the room as I shoved the second half of my sandwich down my throat. The couple began to argue, and around then I realized that a ride home was not going to be in my future.

I opened the front door and walked into the cold Labrador night without a word. Ice crystals formed in my lungs with each breath. My chest tightened as I looked skyward, seeing the aurora borealis for the first time in my life. The northern lights danced to the distant sound of moaning and loud cursing. It wasn't the most magical way to see them but there they were, one shimmering curtain of emerald light.

I had no idea where I was so I kept walking towards the magnificent, otherworldly glimmering beauty. No one could say that I had not tried my best to provide for my little family. I would fly home with a cheque for $500 and a hindquarter of caribou.

As good as Old Joe's bologna sandwich had been, the next sandwich I had was the most exciting meal of my life.

~

In the middle of the night on December 1, 1998, Sherrie turned to me to say she thought her water had broken.

"I'm sure it's nothing," I said, avoiding reality.

"My water definitely broke," she said, with remarkable patience for someone in labour.

"We all have accidents from time to time," I said, trying my best to convince myself that it was not happening. "No need to be embarrassed."

"We have to go to the hospital now," she said, already up and preparing a bag.

I stared at the ceiling, fatherhood looming closer by the second. Our pregnancy course instructor had told us to pack a lunch when Sherrie's water broke because the whole birthing process would take some time and you would get hungry waiting in the hospital. "I better make the sandwich," I said.

I solemnly took two slices of bread from the loaf, added mustard and a slice of bologna as Old Joe had taught me. I sat in the kitchen alone, realizing that the next time I stepped into that room I would be a father.

Sherrie called down from upstairs. "What are you doing?"

"I had to make the sandwich," I answered. It wasn't my fault. The nurse said we had to.

"What's taking you so long?" she asked, pulling her suitcase down the stairs without any help from me.

"I'm eating the sandwich," I answered, and in doing so realized that maybe I was in shock. I could barely put any food on the table, and now that I finally had, I was the one eating it.

Several hours later, Jacob Leo Critch came into this world. The northern lights had nothing on him. His big eyes looked up at me as if to say, "Oh god. You're not a clown, are you? I'm screwed."

I walked home that night once mother and child were settled and sleeping. I needed the air. I wanted to make sure that every opportunity in life was open to Jacob so that he could follow his dreams. But did that mean I would have to give up on mine?

Big round snowflakes fell from the sky. They made lazy circles as they slowly drifted to the ground. As they melted, I felt my dread blossoming into promise. I was not going to let Jacob down. But I wasn't going to let myself down either. I was going to make something of myself. I just had to figure out how.

4

OPPORTUNITY KNOCKS

MANY ACTORS HAVE THE same recurring nightmare. In it, they are onstage in front of an audience with no idea what their lines are. Oftentimes, they have been pushed into the spotlight without even knowing what the play is about. They stand there, with their co-stars staring at them incredulously as they struggle to find the words like a fish on dry land gasping for air. Fatherhood often felt like that for me. In 1999, at the age of twenty-five, I found myself playing a role I was in no way prepared for—dad.

I was drowning in toys, games and comic books. And that was before the kid came. I could barely take care of myself, let alone a helpless child. And so there we were, father and son, staring into each other's eyes, both wondering, "How am I ever going to shepherd this person into adulthood?"

We lived in a tiny rented house in downtown St. John's. It lay right in the middle of the migration path of a large pack of high school kids. A small flock of them would gather right outside of our window at lunchtime to smoke cigarettes and fight over french fries like seagulls in a McDonald's parking lot.

I made the mistake one day of trying to shoo them away. This only angered them more. Each day as I tried to get Jacob to nap they would bang on my front window and shout, "What are ya gonna do, baby-man?" Sometimes I'd throw the door open to scare them off, but they'd just stand there laughing at me. "You can't hit us!" they'd jeer. "We're kids. I'll call the cops on ya, baby-man, ya prick!"

One day when Sherrie came home from work she said, "Somebody spray-painted 'baby-man' on the front of our house!"

"Huh," I replied, trying to hold on to my last shred of pride. "I wonder what that's supposed to mean."

Meanwhile, I started to do commentaries on local CBC Radio. I would make fun of the newsmakers of the week on the morning show, writing them up on the spot whenever I got the call. Being home alone with Jacob made it hard enough to just take the call, let alone write a commentary on short notice.

CBC PRODUCER: Hey, Mark. Mayor Andy Wells just went on another tirade and it's making national news. Can you write something up for tomorrow morning?

Right about then, I would often notice Jacob attempting to pull the TV from the stand.

ME: No, no, no, no, no, no!
CBC PRODUCER: Oh. I'm sorry. I didn't realize you were such a big supporter of Mayor Wells.
ME: No, no, no! I mean yes! Yes! I can do that.
CBC PRODUCER: Great. Can you be here at seven a.m.?

This is when Jacob would traditionally toss pasta sauce onto our white sofa.

ME: Oh, for the love of God!
CBC PRODUCER: Oh. Sorry. That's the only slot we have. I guess we could pre-tape?
ME: No, no, no! That's fine. I'm up then anyway.

Tears begin to flow.

CBC PRODUCER: Is that a baby crying?

ME: No. No. That was me. See you in the morning.

The commentaries were such a success that a local newspaper asked me to write a weekly column for them. People were getting to know me, but my phone still wasn't ringing as often as I needed it to. I suppose there was always a possibility that it had been disconnected. The newspaper job did, however, pay a hundred and fifty bucks per column, and that, combined with the occasional radio commentary, meant I was pulling in a cool five or six hundred bucks a month.

I say "cool" because we still couldn't keep the heat on. For the most part, we were keeping the wolf away from the door, but there were some scratches visible under the doorknob. It was hard to tell if they were from the proverbial wolf or the high school kids that gathered on my step every day.

~

A break isn't worth a damn if you aren't ready for it. You have to learn from every crack and fissure along the way. Sometimes you can spend your whole life beating your head against the wall and the only things that will break are your spirit and your skull.

Every terrible, embarrassing gig along the way prepared me for the call I got in 1999. I was asked to host a fundraiser for the LSPU Hall, the St. John's theatre I first rented when I was just fifteen years old. That small, two-hundred-seat theatre was where many local actors and comedians who went on to national acclaim got their start—including the cast of CBC's political satire *This Hour Has 22 Minutes*. To raise money for much-needed renos, the *22 Minutes* cast were planning a roast of Premier Brian Tobin. I was asked to host the show. I had finally landed a high-profile gig and I was beyond excited.

This Hour Has 22 Minutes had become a national smash hit. The show was filmed in Halifax but its cast and creators were all Newfoundlanders. Mary Walsh struck fear into the hearts of politicians as Marg, Princess Warrior, a riff on the popular *Xena: Warrior Princess* action-adventure TV show of the time. Listening to Rick Mercer's rants had become as much of a national pastime as hockey. Greg Thomey was famous for his iconic characters like Newfoundland separatist politician Jerry Boyle. And Cathy Jones was a chameleon with a spinning prize wheel of hilarious voices.

22 Minutes debuted in 1993. I happened to be in Halifax when the first episode was filmed. I was just out of high school and I travelled to Nova Scotia to perform a sketch comedy show with my friend Paul Edwards in the Atlantic Fringe Festival. I had never seen a city the size of Halifax; to me, it might as well have been New York. The festival paid for our flights, but we didn't have anywhere to stay. "We'll figure it out when we get there," I said, never having been off the island before.

Lucky for me, Paul had been unlucky in love. A recent engagement had fallen through and his fiancée had returned the ring. Paul brought it with him and he decided to hock it to keep us in beer and burgers. To hell with failed romances, we had failing careers to worry about.

We crashed on the floor of the apartment of a childhood friend of Paul's with the solemn oath that we would be gone the next night. We performed our sketches to a full house, pulling costumes from a suitcase onstage that had not been unpacked since we left St. John's. Most of our material had not been performed before an audience either. We were under-rehearsed and overly nervous, but what we lacked in experience, we made up for in panicked adrenaline.

The next day we sat on a park bench to read the review in the local paper. We had no idea what to expect, but we were working for a cut of the door, so a good review was the difference between making the cab fare to get to the airport and walking there. I was too nervous to look, so I made Paul read it to me. I turned my gaze to the next bench where an old man was feeding bread to some pigeons and marvelled at how even the birds were better fed than I was.

"Okay, here goes," Paul said, opening the paper. "'Laugh-out-loud hilarious and immensely irreverent. Edwards and Critch offer a fast-paced 50 minutes of wry, biting humour. Let's hope the local CBC TV execs drop down to see this show. The writing is crisp, the talent is strong, and pacing and material would fit 11 p.m.'"

I hopped up on the bench and danced a hearty jig.

"You're scaring the birds," the elderly birder chastised. I shouted my apologies as we ran down the path and onto the street of the once distant land that we had now conquered and claimed as our own.

One of the many great things about being a Newfoundlander is that wherever you are in the world, you will run into another Newfoundlander. There was a Newfoundlander with Lincoln at Gettysburg. Squanto, the Native American who served as a guide to the Pilgrim settlers at Plymouth, learned English in Newfoundland. And here, walking towards us on a sunny street in Halifax, was Rick Mercer.

We exchanged the traditional greeting of our people.

"What are ya at, Rick?"

"What are you at, Mark?"

Rick congratulated us on our review and then one-upped us. He told us that he was going to be part of the cast of a six-episode summer series on CBC TV. It was going to be a weekly roundup of the news headlines co-starring Mary Walsh, Greg Thomey and Cathy Jones.

I didn't think, *Wow! This is lucky. The review even stated explicitly that the CBC execs should hire us! Maybe I should ask for a writing gig!* I thought, *Hmmm. I wonder if Rick has a couch.* Rick kindly let us crash on the floor of his apartment for the rest of the run.

Weeks later, I stood in a pub watching the debut of *22 Minutes*, trying to shush the crowd around me. There was Rick, on national TV, doing sketch comedy. I couldn't believe it. He had made it.

~

It wasn't until six years later, when I hosted the roast of Premier Brian Tobin, that I actually found myself working alongside the cast of *22 Minutes*. In the back of my mind, I thought that if the show at the LSPU Hall went well, then maybe, just maybe, I would get a second shot at writing for *22 Minutes*.

Tickets were two hundred bucks each and the ballroom was sold out. Everyone was excited to see the cast of local heroes perform in person, but there was something missing. Rick was a no-show, and rumours began to swirl that he was quitting *22 Minutes*. I filled in for him that night at the roast, playing the straight man in one of their sketches. The night was a smashing success, but I was happiest for getting the three-course dinner and two drink tickets. When I went home, I couldn't help but hear a nagging voice that said, "If Rick leaves, maybe you will get the job." That voice belonged to my father.

"Good god, Mark!" he shouted in a gravelly voice well sanded with constant applications of Rothmans cigarettes and coffee. "You can do that job. It's only making faces! Do you want me to make some calls? I know people at CBC. The guy who does the weather is a personal friend."

My mother was also a great comfort. Whenever I dropped little Jacob off so I could write, she would gently encourage me in her usual machine-gun-fire blitzkrieg blast of perpetual speech.

"My-god-Mark-why-don't-you-let-your-father-call-the-weatherman-now-and-see-if-there's-a-job-posting-for-TV-host-before-some-frigger-from-the-mainland-gets-the-job?"

I tried to explain to her that hosting a TV show isn't the kind of thing that you could call first dibs on. I put any thoughts of national TV away and went back to worrying about what local gig was going to pay for diapers.

Sherrie gently suggested I apply for unemployment insurance (by then more optimistically called employment insurance) until I could figure something out. I felt defeated and a little humiliated but what could I do? Maybe it was time to give up on my foolish, selfish dream.

Realizing that my number was up, I went to the UI office and took a number. I took my place in the waiting room and hoped I wouldn't be recognized, though, if I had been recognizable, I wouldn't have needed UI.

I sat down next to a silver-haired man, nervously tapping his cigarette pack on his knee like a woodpecker with a jackhammer. "Number seventy-six," he muttered. "I'm going to be here all packin' day!" He wore paint-covered overalls and well-scuffed workboots. He seemed to be after a more traditional type of employment. He tapped me on the arm and motioned towards the civil servant behind the desk.

"He don't care about us," he said, more to himself than to me. "I've been waiting here over an hour. He's just treading water now until he gets his fat pension from our tax dollars!"

I nodded, despite the fact that I was clearly not paying many taxes. "I know, right?" I shook my head and folded my arms in disgust to commiserate with my fellow out-of-working-class hero. "Probably never swung a hammer in his life."

"You work construction?" he asked, impressed.

"Not exactly," I said as I dug my hands deeper beneath my armpits to hide my perfectly manicured nails and marshmallow-soft palms.

"Landscaper?" he asked.

I shook my head. "Allergies." My eyes darted back to the sign that informed me they were now serving number sixty-two.

"I don't like to talk about work," I said, hoping to change the topic. "I mean, I bet you don't like thinking about your old job, either."

"Heavy equipment technician," he said, more than happy to talk about his life's passion. "Bulldozers, graders, worked it all. Blades, side booms, didn't matter. Then they tell me they don't need me anymore. Downsizing. Pricks. What kind of work did you say you were in?"

"I'm an actor," I mumbled.

He sat upright as if I had just told him that I killed puppies for a living. "What do you mean, actor?" he asked, loud enough to cause a few of the heads around us to turn in our direction. "You must have a real job too, don't ya?"

"Acting is a real job," I gently protested. "I'm just . . . between projects."

"You hear this?" he shouted to the man sitting across from us. "Burt Reynolds here is looking for his UI."

I imagined my number being called. I would be humiliated a second time, but with the added joy of paperwork. I stood up and walked out, a trail of laughter following behind me. Not only could I not get a job,

I couldn't even be successfully unemployed. But at least I was finally getting some laughs.

~

"Good god!" my father bellowed from the other end of the phone line. "Did you read the news? Mercer quit! Get down to the CBC building and ask for Karl, the weatherman!"

"Call-them-up-and-ask-them-if-you-can-drop-off-a-résumé-Mark," my mother howled in the background like an air-raid siren at Pearl Harbor.

It was true. Rick had announced that he was leaving. He was writing and starring in a new sitcom called *Made in Canada*. Everywhere I went, people were telling me, "You should take that Rick Mercer job," as if it was as simple as walking into the studio with the Help Wanted sign in the window and asking, "Still hiring?"

I started to get calls from the local newspapers, radio shows and magazines all asking me the same question: "Are you going to take over from Rick Mercer?" The articles often quoted "sources" that had "heard" that I was being considered for—or even already had—the job. I called a friend who worked at a radio station and asked him who their mystery source was. "Your father," he told me. "I just assumed he was speaking on your behalf." I went straight to the house, and Dad confessed. I was furious and begged him to stop.

"Stop?" he shouted as he exhaled a third of a year off his life from his nostrils and bit into a cookie like a diabetic dragon. "Don't you know show business? There's no such thing as bad press. If you print it, it's true! I just got off the phone with a contact at the *Buy and Sell* magazine. They're interested in a chat with you for their 'What's Happening' feature. That reminds me. I'm selling the old couch. Give me a hand getting it to the curb."

"Please stop doing this," I begged. "I'm not going to get that job and you'll have hyped everyone up for no reason. You're building expectations that I can't possibly meet. You're setting me up to fail!"

"Fine," my father said, rolling his eyes so far back up into his head that I wondered for a moment if they would get stuck and I'd have to take him to an optometrist to have them professionally rolled back down. "I won't tell anyone else about your new job."

"I don't *have* a new job!" I shouted, my words bouncing off him like rubber balls off a tank.

My mother spun my son around the room, saying, "You-hear-that-Jacob? Daddy-is-gonna-be-on-TV-but-we-can't-tell-anybody." *Great*, I thought, *the disappointment in me is going to be multi-generational.*

I did not believe in myself the way my parents believed in me, but it turns out I should have. *22 Minutes* asked me to send in a demo tape.

I called my best friend, Tristy Clark. He was a videographer and had all the gear you needed back then to make a tape: cameras, wires, videotapes, microphones, an editing suite, lighting. Basically, everything you now have in the smartphone in your pocket. Tristy had an hour between shoots for his real job and, if I hurried, we could just bang out an audition in time.

I tore through a newspaper and hastily wrote some material while Tristy transformed a bedroom into a TV set.

"Hello and welcome to *This Audition Tape Has 5 Minutes*. I'm not Rick Mercer," I somewhat shyly, and far too honestly, began. I then jumped right into some topical desk jokes—these are short jokes told from a news desk that comment on the latest stories—before doing a character piece . . .

My father had been adamant that I use the local weatherman to get the job and so I took his advice, but in a roundabout way. After all, what's a news show without the weather report? I introduced myself from the desk.

"Well, no news is good news but no clothes is great news," I said. "The website nakednews.com, which features female anchors slowly undressing as they report the news, recently added its first male anchor. The CBC, never wanting to fall behind, recently added its first nude weatherman. Here he is now, Skip Bambraugh. Skip?"

We then cut to me, outside. I stepped out onto the deck, wearing a powder blue suit, my hair slicked to one side in a bad comb-over, with the St. John's Harbour in the background.

"Thank you, Rick," I said in a quivering voice that was part character and part nerves. "Uh, Skip Bambraugh here with the weather, coming to you live from the East Coast. I have to say, I'm not too comfortable with this whole nudity thing, but a weatherman will do what he has to do to bring the weather to the country."

I then began to undress, slowly peeling off my jacket and unbuttoning my shirt. It was then that I noticed the high school kids walking their way back down the street in their usual wolf pack. I picked up the pace of my speech, hoping that my audition tape wouldn't end with me being bullied by the kids.

"It's a very hot summer. Some might say sweltering, and now the weatherman is going to make it even hotter for the ladies." As my shirt and tie came off, I revealed that I had drawn a weather map of the island of Newfoundland on my chest and stomach with a Sharpie.

From the corner of my eye I could see the tallest of the herd of street urchins point at the baby-man shooting a topless video. The pack began to run towards me.

"Now we are going to take an in-depth look at the rock, and no," I continued, "I don't mean my abs. I mean the island of Newfoundland." I began to rub my nipple. "Okay, up here by my nipple, on the Avalon Peninsula, it's very hot and sultry. Now, moving across the island portion of the province, it's getting a little bit warmer there, too."

The kids were getting closer now, and I felt a little like Indiana Jones desperately trying to stay ahead of the giant boulder as it rolled towards him. At this point, my nerdy weatherman began to pant a little. "But the best part? The best part? The best part is down on the Southern Shore," I said, gesturing to the part of the island hidden by my pants. "If you're in the area, I can guarantee you, there's a one hundred percent chance of precipitation down there tonight!"

We then cut back to me at the desk, as the anchor. "Thank you for the opportunity and, uh, talk to you later. Bye." I ducked back inside, slamming the door and denying the gang of street kids of their prey. Tristy made a copy of the tape and I submitted the package. There was nothing left to do but wait.

~

My phone eventually rang, a month later, in July. But it was not *22 Minutes* calling. It was my friend Shaun Majumder. Shaun was going to host part of Canada's—and the world's—biggest comedy festival, Just For Laughs, and he wanted me to come to Montreal and write for him.

Each night, when our work was done, I would stand in the wings of the Saint-Denis Theatre and watch some of the greatest acts in the world hone their craft: Howie Mandel, Dave Chappelle, Jim Gaffigan, Jeffrey Ross, Jimmy Carr, Chris Rock, Carl Reiner and on and on and on. The after-parties would go on until sunrise. I remember chatting about silent film stars one night on the balcony of a hotel room with Jerry Seinfeld's legendary agent George Shapiro while Mitch Hedberg happily slept in the bathtub. I felt like I had stepped through the looking glass. First Trinity, then Halifax and now Montreal. I was slowly wading deeper into the water but I was still terrified of drowning.

It was when I was at Just For Laughs that I got the call my father had been predicting. The *22 Minutes* producers wanted me to fly to Toronto to audition in person. I ran down the narrow backstage hallway of the Saint-Denis Theatre to find Shaun and tell him the good news. Comics nervously paced back and forth like racehorses in a barn.

"Guess what," Shaun shouted when he saw me. "I just got a call from *22 Minutes*. They want me to audition to replace Rick." And with that, my big break was broken in two.

~

I caught my first glimpse of the CN Tower from the window of an Air Canada plane as it coasted down to the runway. Growing up, Toronto had seemed to me a strange alien world where Wayne and Shuster wore tuxedos and the Leafs perpetually lost. But there was no time for sightseeing. I dropped my bag at the hotel and headed across town to a warehouse where the auditions were taking place.

Shaun was on the audition list, and so was comedian Gavin Crawford. Gavin had received critical acclaim for his Comedy Network program aptly titled *The Gavin Crawford Show*. He was armed with a bevy of characters and accents that made him a perfect choice for the show. Talk show host and future member of Parliament Seamus O'Regan was also in the running, plus a few others. It was a pretty stacked deck.

We each performed a prepared piece in front of leading producer, or showrunner, Mark Farrell and executive producer and show owner, Michael Donovan. Farrell was a respected stand-up comedian, and a longtime *22 Minutes* writer, well known for his hilarious performance alongside Jeremy Hotz in the classic Ken Finkleman series *The Newsroom*. Donovan had produced the *22 Minutes* predecessor *CODCO* series and had won an Academy Award for the Michael Moore documentary *Bowling for Columbine*. I was intimidated but confident that this was in my wheelhouse. I was going to give it my best shot.

They threw us a curve ball. We all received a news story and were asked to go in the next room to write a monologue about it. They asked me to write my monologue from the point of view of an NDP MP from British Columbia giving his thoughts on a recent strike in the area. We were given twenty minutes to write something up before performing it in front of the stone-faced executives.

This might have been intimidating to a lot of people, but for me it was second nature. Gavin was a chameleon. Shaun was a comedic dynamo who practically dripped charm. But writing topical comedy on the spot was my strength. I was easily the least well known of the three, but I was getting my chance to show them what I could do. I sat down and focused. I searched my memory for everything I could remember about BC. I thought about strikes. Funny chants and picket signs. I put down my pen. I was done in fifteen minutes.

"That was quick," Donovan said with a look of surprise. I began to wonder if I should have spent more time on it. Maybe I was going to come off as cocky.

"Okay," Mark said. "Let's see what you've got."

I performed my piece with the confidence of a man who had nothing to lose. I got a laugh right away and that eased my nerves. As I finished, I could see that they were impressed that I could deliver jokes with such a quick turnaround.

Next, they asked me what I would do differently with the show—what did I like and what would I change. My mouth grew dry. This was a land mine that I did not want to step on. These people decided what went in the show. To criticize it was to criticize them. My mind went blank.

Plus, I hadn't exactly been a faithful viewer of the show. These days, I was more likely to be found watching *Sesame Street* than a show that satirized Canadian politics. I sat there like an idiot and I couldn't even remember how many minutes an hour was supposed to have.

"Come on," Michael said with a smile. "Anything at all."

The only thing I could think of was Rick Mercer's segment, "Talking to Americans."

"What about 'Talking to Mexicans'?" I asked, as a joke.

"Thanks for coming in," Michael said, looking at me the way a vegan might stare at a butcher's smock.

I went back to Newfoundland, pretty sure that I had blown it.

~

A few weeks later, my parents banged on my door with a frenzy usually reserved to tell people that their house is on fire. "My-god-that-crowd-played-a-dirty-trick-on-you," my mother said as she blew past me to fill the kettle. This was a surefire sign that a serious conversation was coming.

"The bastards screwed us," my old man said, tossing a newspaper down on the table.

I opened it up to find a giant picture of *Whose Line Is It Anyway?* star Colin Mochrie. If you looked up "ubiquitous" in the dictionary in those days, you would have seen a picture of Colin Mochrie. He was a huge star. And he was most certainly not a Newfoundlander.

"Mary," my father ordered in a tone used by generals in wartime, "call the paper and cancel our subscription."

Filling Rick's shoes was a big gamble for the 22 brass, and rightfully so they went with the biggest name they could find in Canadian show business. I licked my wounds and carried on as normal.

Before long, though, I got a call from Mark Farrell, the show-runner who'd overseen my audition. He offered me a chance to come in as a writer for two weeks. I was getting another shot. I didn't want to get everyone's hopes up, so I only told Sherrie and my parents, calling them up and begging them not to tell anyone this time. Before I hung up the phone, an article appeared in the *Newfoundland Herald*.

THIS HOUR RECRUITS CRITCH

Mark Critch has been temporarily hired as a writer with the CBC's award-winning television comedy *This Hour Has 22 Minutes*. Critch, a talented comic, writer and actor, who hails from the province's capital, was contacted by producers of the show last week.

Thanks, Dad.

5

THIS CHAPTER
HAS 22 MINUTES

ON MY FIRST DAY AT WORK, I stood outside the CBC building in Halifax pacing back and forth, smoking to ease my nerves. I'm ashamed to admit it now, but I smoked for ten years. I had started smoking for a play. Each time I lit a cigarette in rehearsal, the smoke would go into my eyes, causing me to cry. Whenever we went for a pint, I would ask my friend Tristy to join me outside for some smoking practice. I got pretty good at it too. By the time the curtain was up on the play I looked like I was a real smoker. That's because I was one. I found myself going for pints just so I could have a smoke. I smoked on my way to the pub and on the way back. I smoked on the front step and on the back porch. Or in the basement with a window open. Or inside. But I wasn't addicted.

And in the CBC parking lot, I smoked both for my nerves and to kill time. I had been so worried about being late that I showed up an hour early for work. I noticed a small group of CBC cameramen smoking off by a loading bay. Smokers lived on the edges, in the alleys and decks and back steps. We were all smokers, and being such, were bound by an unspoken oath to make small talk with each other. I wasn't in the mood for small talk, but I knew from my days playing theatres that it was a good idea to get in with the crew. If they liked you, they would probably laugh at your jokes. And if you could make the crew laugh, you could make anyone laugh. They had seen it all.

"I'm the new writer," I said as I joined them.

Their eyes searched me up and down like World War II searchlights trying to find an enemy bomber over London. I was wearing my best shirt and a pair of dress pants. I looked like I was going to the wedding of someone I didn't know very well. I was even wearing new shoes that I had bought at Payless the night before. Though they were half a size too big, they didn't feel so bad in the store. But now, whenever I took more than a couple of steps, my left heel would pop out.

The crew guys continued their chat without me. They had seen fresh-faced comics like me fed into their meat grinder before. They kept to themselves in a kind of "best not to start naming the farm animals" kind of way.

I finished my smoke and slowly shuffled into the building like Frankenstein's monster. I opened the door and there I was, working on a national TV show. There was, however, no time to enjoy the moment. I rushed into the washroom and jammed some tissue into the toe of each shoe, securing my footwear and ensuring I didn't accidentally kick someone in the head from across the room on my first day.

The *22 Minutes* offices were not what you would call flashy. The show had been a CBC staple for eleven years, but the whole place seemed like a camp set up by carnies while the fair was in town for the weekend.

Mark Farrell, show-runner, received me politely, the way he might sign for a package he had been expecting. He took me straight into the writers' room. A giant window made up most of the wall that faced the corridor, so that the room looked like an aquarium for people. Four battered desks lined the walls. Three of them were occupied by guys who all wore jeans and T-shirts. I was overdressed.

I confidently strode towards my desk to mask my embarrassment. In doing so, I accidentally kicked one of my oversized loafers across the room. It wedged itself between the desk and the heater and I took my seat, having somehow managed to show up for work both over-dressed and partially barefoot.

Mark introduced me to the others and gave me the lay of the land. "This is Peter McBain," he said, pointing to a guy my age with thick glasses that made him seem wise beyond his years. Years later, Peter would take the reins as executive producer of *22 Minutes* himself. If our writers' room had been the team in a heist movie, McBain would be the guy with the blueprints to the vault and the stopwatch. He looked smart. He was even smarter than he looked.

"That's Kevin." Mark pointed to a sweet-faced blond man. Kevin White was a comic from Ontario. He thrust his hand out in the way of a Mormon missionary. There was something calming about his eager friendliness, and I immediately felt at ease. Kevin would go on to co-create the hit CBC sitcom *Kim's Convenience*. In the heist movie, Kevin would be the face of the organization, gaining our crew access to the casino through sheer charm.

"And that's Paul Mather," Farrell said, finishing his introductions. Paul was an Albertan improvisational comic. Paul was a joke machine, hardly ever looking up from his laptop. He was destined to head south to write and produce American sitcoms. He took his job seriously and put a sketch together the way a mechanic would repair a transmission. In the heist movie, Paul would be the munitions expert tasked with blowing the vault wide open. He never failed.

"Guys, this is new Keith," Farrell announced to a laugh.

Peter explained, "Keith was the guy who used to have your desk."

"He didn't make it," Farrell said nonchalantly.

Make what? Was he dead?

"He didn't get picked up after his two-week trial," Kevin said. "It happens." I would be sitting in a dead man's chair. I felt like I had been given a bed in a hospital ward and it was still warm.

"Okay, time for the ideas meeting," Farrell said, abruptly ending my orientation session. Things moved at a clip there. If you didn't paddle, you would surely be swept over the falls.

"Every week there's an ideas meeting," Kevin briefed me as we walked down a hallway to a large meeting room. "You need to write four sketches and ten desk jokes. If some of them are funny they'll make it into the book. That's a big script that the cast reads in front of most of the company."

"We call that the Humilitorium," Peter elaborated. "It's not fun to sit there while your sketch bombs." I loved an optimist.

"It's not so bad," said Paul. The golden boy had no worry of bombing.

The Humilitorium reminded me of the president's Situation Room. It was cavernous and dark, with large fluorescent lights that hung directly over a long, white table. I was a little intimidated to see the cast sitting there. Mary Walsh hopped up to give me a hug.

"Mark," she said in voice familiar to just about every Canadian. "It's so good to have you here, darling. I told them we just had to get you. You're so funny, dear!" I was relieved to get the compliment but burdened by the pressure. A moment before I was just a new writer that nobody expected to last two weeks. Now I was guaranteed to be funny by the star of the show.

I took a seat next to Mary and opened my notepad. I looked around the room and quickly realized that I was the only writer sitting at the table.

"Writers sit against the wall," Paul told me with a smile. "Cast, producers and department heads at the table."

I had suffered my first humiliation in the Humilitorium. I went and sat next to Kevin, and he whispered a play-by-play in my ear.

"There's two types of sketches," he explained. "They shoot around six sketches in the studio or on location. Two or three are taped on the night of the live taping in front of the audience. They have to take place on set. Living room, kitchen, whatever."

Farrell went around the room and called on each of us to pitch an idea. Peter, Kevin and Paul each threw out idea after idea, like kids at batting practice. The cast started to riff on some of the things they had suggested and most of their jokes were home runs. Sketches were practically being written in front of my eyes. I stayed in the outfield and played with my glove, hoping no one would throw the ball to me.

They seemed to forget me as they headed home, buzzing with ideas. I sat alone, staring into the stark white blankness of my notepad, my head as empty as the room.

That night I sat in my room with a stack of newspapers, carefully cutting out the stories that I thought would work as sketches.

I had watched my father perform this same ritual each night before supper. While Mom prepared the meal, Dad would lie on his bed smoking behind the newspaper. On his stomach lay a pair of big silver scissors. They looked more like something a mayor would use to snip the ceremonial ribbon at a new grocery store than a writer's tool. I remember standing in the doorway as a kid, watching Dad, his face obscured by the paper until the single blade of a pair of scissors would poke through the page. A few more snips and a rectangle of paper would fall, revealing his face and a puff of a smoke.

Dad would stuff his articles into bulging manila envelopes. I'd often find him furiously pulling yellowed paper from his stack, muttering to himself, hoping to find some detail in a story that could prove or disprove some freshly reported nugget, linking the facts together, until he had a noose with which to hang his subject.

Now here I was, lighting cigarettes off the dying embers of their comrades as I combed through the newspapers looking for something, anything, to write a joke about. We didn't have the internet in the writers' room and I sure didn't have it in my apartment. I became my own search engine, combing the paper for jokes with scissors like a caveman.

The next day, I passed in my sketches like a nervous fifth grader expecting to fail math. To pass the time before the next meeting in the Humilitorium, I decided to draw some cartoons on the whiteboard in the writers' room. I took the top off a marker and doodled cartoon versions of some CBC stars. I was pretty happy with my handiwork and stood back to admire it.

"That's not a dry erase marker," Peter McBain said from behind me. "It's a Sharpie. You just ruined the whiteboard." I frantically scrubbed at Rick Mercer's cartoon head to no avail. "It's time for the meeting," Peter added on his way out the door. At least my day couldn't get any worse.

All three of the sketches I had written were chosen to be taped live in front of the audience. I had a comedy hat trick! Not a bad first week. The arts department, costumes, and hair and makeup went right to work like Santa's elves on Christmas Eve. I peeked into the studio as the crew assembled sets, turning four-by-eight flats and windows into rooms I had only imagined the night before.

On show night, the writers would usually watch the show on a monitor in the safety of the Humilitorium. But I wanted to hear the laughs first-hand. I sat amongst the crowd, like a downed pilot behind enemy lines.

My first sketch starred Colin Mochrie as a Canada Post worker. I had found an article about an ossuary that supposedly held the bones of Jesus's brother James. It had been damaged in the mail en route to a Canadian museum. The audience did not care much for the sight of someone bashing the bones of Christ's brother, however. I watched in terror as Colin struggled to ignite my lines with some comedic fire, but the wick was damp. He was bombing.

All that money, all that time, wasted. Surely one of the other writers' scripts would have worked better than this. Was I in trouble? I wondered if I should offer to pay for all the lumber used to make the set.

The crew wheeled away the post office set and pushed in the living room set for my next sketch. For a moment I considered escaping backstage, but then I would have to face the guys who had surely watched my skit bomb on the monitor. Not to mention Colin, who was surely having his wig and makeup removed like a knight being extricated from his armour after a sad defeat.

In my next sketch, Greg Thomey played a twenty-something who wouldn't leave the nest. I had carefully snipped out a story that said more and more young people were choosing to stay at home rather than move out on their own. The sketch began with Cathy Jones complaining about having her grown son underfoot. Greg, upset by being dubbed a freeloader, decides to leave home, slamming the door behind him. He instantly returns, crying because he fell and skinned his knee.

Cathy comforts him on her lap and ties his shoelace for him. Crisis averted. The audience loved it.

That skit was going in the show, but I was focused on the ones that didn't. I can't say they made the wrong decision, though. Even I can't remember what my third sketch was about, so clearly it wasn't that memorable!

That night, I lay awake in my bed. There was no time to feel smug about my success. I tossed and turned, wondering what the hell I was going to write about the next day when the whole process would begin again.

I had only been hired for a two-week trial and now my time was up. I went into Farrell's office and timidly asked if it was okay to come back on Monday. He looked at me like I was crazy as he swung an imaginary golf club in the air. "What? Yes. Of course! They'll just extend you or whatever. How's this swing look to you?"

~

I flew back home for a visit and was given a hero's welcome by my family. Time slips by in seconds, but when you're a parent you count time in inches. Jacob seemed to have grown half a foot in the short time I had been gone. I had missed those precious inches of his childhood and my pride soon turned to guilt. Jacob was growing fast, and every time I came back, that change manifested itself in some new way. Juice cups were passé; he was a glass man now. Stuffed toys were for babies; he was a truck man. Every time I saw him, some new achievement had been unlocked like a character in a video game.

My son wasn't the only one who changed since I left. My father, at the age of eighty, told me that he had decided to quit smoking.

"How old were you when you started?" I asked.

"Twelve," he answered as he buttered a raisin bun.

"Why now, after almost seventy years?" I asked.

"Because Doctor Bob said it would be a good idea." Dad seemed almost annoyed at the stupidity of the question. He finished the tea bun and began to butter another. I was beginning to see what his new vice would be.

"But won't it be difficult?" I asked, wondering which was worse for you, a pack of smokes or a package of tea buns a day.

"It's the hardest thing I've ever had to do. Good god! What's wrong with you?" The last sentence was obscured by a mouthful of baked carbs covered in a dollop of heart attack, but at least he wasn't smoking.

"Then why quit?" I asked.

"Because the man asked me to and I said I would. I gave him my word."

And that was that. He made a promise and he kept it. No patch. No gum. No vaporizer. Just his word.

I wondered, If he could do it, could I? I decided to give it a try.

My father's generation was made of tougher stuff than mine. He was made of the kind of stuff that you reach for when you fall. Steel. Wood. Iron. My generation was made of the kind of stuff that would come crashing to the ground with you. Plastic. Polyester. Kraft cheese slices. For me, it was nowhere near as easy as it had been for my father. I'd have a puff to hold off my craving, another puff when I got my craving and a third puff to reward myself for getting through the craving. Soon, I was smoking more while quitting than I had when I was a smoker.

I missed the smokers even more than I missed the smokes. There seemed to be no escaping my fellow addicts. If I turned my gaze away from the pack of smokers outside our studio, my eyes would fall upon a guy at the hospital next door. He would lift his oxygen mask, take a draw, exhale, lower the mask and then repeat. There's no more Canadian sight than a person in a bathrobe standing in a snowbank outside a hospital lighting smokes off their oxygen tank. We shared a nod, and for a moment I didn't know whether I envied him or pitied him.

I reached for my smokes. I thought of my dad. I tossed the pack into a garbage can and reached into my other pocket. I unwrapped a chocolate bar and waddled my way into work.

Like me, *22 Minutes* was at a crossroads then, as it often has been over its twenty-eight-year history. Whenever I told someone that I worked on the show, they would invariably ask, "Is Rick Mercer still on that show?" On the rare occasion when they didn't, they would say, "I haven't watched it since Rick left," as if it was a badge of honour.

Colin needed a breakout piece, but he wasn't really made for a show like *22 Minutes*. Political satire often comes with a dash of meanness, and Colin is the most lovable person on earth. Colin couldn't replace Rick. That was impossible. What we had to do was find a way to write for Colin's voice and make it work for the show.

Colin happened to be in Washington, DC, for a *Whose Line* event, and the *22 Minutes* producers decided to send a camera down to see if they could piggyback off it. Rick's "Talking to Americans" pieces had become iconic, and we had to be careful not to tread on them. This was going to have to be something different.

We settled on the idea of a monologue shot around the landmarks of the National Mall. We went around the room with each of the writers contributing a paragraph for Colin to deliver as an insincere apology to Americans. The piece combined Colin's sweetness and Canada's reputation for apologizing into a double-edged blade to twist into the hearts of our southern neighbours.

"On behalf of Canadians everywhere," he began, speaking straight into the camera, "I'd like to offer an apology to the United States of America. We haven't been getting along very well recently, and for that I am truly sorry."

"I'm sorry about our waffling on Iraq," he said. "I mean, when you're going up against a crazed dictator, you want to have your friends by your side. I realize it took more than two years before you guys pitched in against Hitler, but that was different. Everyone knew he had weapons." Then he paused in front of the White House.

"I'm sorry we burned down your White House during the War of 1812," he said with a contrite smile. "I see you've rebuilt it! It's very nice."

"And finally, on behalf of all Canadians," he concluded, "I'm sorry that we're constantly apologizing for things in a passive-aggressive way which is really a thinly veiled criticism. I sincerely hope that you're not upset over this. Because we've seen what you do to countries you get upset with."

When the piece played back in front of the audience they roared with approval. The internet was still a novelty, but someone typed up the text of the piece and it found its way onto message boards and internet newsgroups around the country. We had a viral hit. The show had suffered a potentially mortal blow when Rick left, but now it was finding its feet again.

I was finding my footing as well. Towards the end of the season I finally got a chance to show my stuff on-camera. The Nokia Brier was taking place in Halifax that year, and the city was filled with curling fans who had come from all around the country to cheer on the men as they competed for the title. Greg Thomey was supposed to cover the event but, as the shooting schedule changed, he became unavailable. Mark Farrell asked me if I wanted to give it a shot. Of course I wanted to! This was Canadian show business, and I was going to get my big break at a curling match. Could there be a better omen?

I started my piece from up in the stands, surrounded by fans. "Excited fans here, desperately trying to stay awake. Not only is it nine thirty in the morning, they're watching curling." I managed to get into the dressing room area, where we persuaded the Quebec skip, Guy Hemmings, to give us an interview.

"Right now, here we are with Guy Hemmings, the Gretzky, the Tiger Woods of curling. Mr. Hemmings, how about an autograph?" I asked, pen and paper in hand. Guy smiled, delighted with the praise. "And who will I make it out to?" I asked, signing my own name. Thankfully he laughed, and I had my first joke.

Next, I managed to persuade the Newfoundland and Labrador skip, Brad Gushue, to play. The province had just changed its official name from Newfoundland to Newfoundland and Labrador, so I used that to launch into my scene.

"The Newfoundland now the Newfoundland AND Labrador team, does that bother you? It's a long name, hard to cheer. Give me an N, give me an E, give me a W, give me an F, give me an O, give me a U, give me an N, give me D, give me an L, give me an A, give me an N, give me a D, give me an L, give me an A, give me a B, give me an R, give me an A, give me a D, give me an O, give me an R! Kind of hard. The official name of the province now being Newfoundland AND Labrador, how does that play into things? Are you worried about the dogs? If you have a Newfoundland dog, is that now a Newfoundland AND Labrador dog? If you have a Labrador retriever, is that now a Newfoundland AND Labrador retriever? And if you have a Newfoundland/ Lab mix, is that now a Newfoundland and Labrador/Newfoundland and Labrador dog or what?"

Brad is one of the nicest, quietest, soft-tempered people you could ever meet. He stood there smiling, not sure what to say next, but doing his best to be supportive. I had my second beat.

Brad would go on to win Olympic gold but he would not be the only person there to one day represent Canada on the global stage. Stephen Harper was the leader of the Canadian Alliance party at the time. He had come to the brier to schmooze, to support Alberta and, like me, to pretend to enjoy curling. He would go on to become Canada's twenty-second prime minister, but back then he was just an Opposition leader who needed press.

He was sitting in the stands with a big Albertan flag so I approached him with a large Newfoundland and Labrador flag.

"Stephen Harper. You never know who you're going to find at curling. Now, you're the leader of a political party, I'm a CBC sports journalist. Of course, we both have to remain objective and completely unbiased here at the game." I jumped up on my feet and started to wave my flag and yell "Newfoundlaaaaaand!"

Harper played along, jumping up with his flag and screaming "Alberta rules!" We began waving our flags in each other's faces. I screamed "Newfoundland!" at the top of my lungs and wrapped my flag around Harper's head, pushing him back into his seat. Stephen

Harper once referred to Atlantic Canada as a place having a "culture of defeat," but that night he helped me win. I had my first road piece, and I became the roving correspondent for the show.

Not long after, Mary Walsh decided to take a leave of absence. She, like Rick before her, had sold another series to CBC and would be busy writing and filming it. While she was away, her chair became a rotating guest slot. They brought in Shaun Majumder to try out for a couple of weeks. His sweaty Raj Binder character soon became a favourite. Alberta's Gavin Crawford came in and killed with a sketch in which he portrayed a two-faced politician as Gollum from *Lord of the Rings*.

At the end of my second season, I finally got my shot, thanks to Air Canada. Colin Mochrie was stuck in Las Vegas and he might not be able to make it back in time for the *22 Minutes* taping. There was a lot of talk about what to do. Shoot around him? Just do the show with the three available cast?

At one point, our costume designer opened the door and asked me what size suit I wore. "Medium?" I guessed, trying to sound cultured. She ran a tape measure around me and disappeared. In most professions, a co-worker measuring your inseam at your desk might set off some red flags. But I had joined the circus. All of the writers would occasionally be called in to play a background character, so this wasn't all that unusual.

It wasn't until around seven that night, when I was leaving, that it struck me. As I was making my way out the door, Siobhan, our production coordinator, said, "You seem pretty calm. Good for you."

"Pardon me?" I asked, unsure what I should be nervous about other than fatherhood, a life in the arts and tripping in my ridiculous footwear.

"You're going on the desk tomorrow to replace Colin," she said matter-of-factly. "Didn't they tell you?"

"Oh, that," I replied, trying to hide my own shock. "Oh yes. Of course. Should be fun. Good night."

Nobody had told me. Looking back, I could see that it had been alluded to. Suggested. Implied. I had even been measured for a suit.

But I had been too stupid to pick up on any of that. I shuffled back to my apartment and called home. I was getting my shot.

~

The next day was a whirlwind of rehearsals and costume fittings. I got a haircut. I put on a suit and I tried my best to exude confidence. Everything had been building up to this moment for me: the sketch shows in high school, the time spent learning my craft in Trinity, performing in gymnatoriums across eastern Canada, and of course the hours and hours of getting a feel for the show in the writing room. But I still couldn't help but wonder if I was ready, even after all of that. Would my big break end up breaking me? There was only one way to find out.

The audience came in and was informed that I would be filling in for Colin Mochrie. I heard a sigh of disappointment. The familiar theme music played. The camera pushed into me on the news desk in my new suit, and I was off.

Later in the night, I played opposite Cathy Jones in a sketch that had been written by Paul Mather. Violence among parents attending their children's hockey games had become a problem, and we played a husband and wife currently under indictment for hockey rage.

CATHY: Well, you know, this is all a misunderstanding. It's just his way of speaking.

MARK: Well, maybe I said some things I shouldn't have but you know it's hard. Your son's out there, it's the third period of the game and you want to tell him, COME ON! GET IN THERE AND KNOCK SOME HEADS! AND THEN THE STUPID BLIND REF CALLS HIM FOR BLUFFING? ARE YOU INSANE? THE OTHER KID STARTED IT!

Then I started to swear, my words bleeped for TV, as I flipped the chair and started pounding on the kitchen table of our set. The punch came when Greg, as the news anchor interviewing us, suggested I see a psychologist.

MARK: Oh, I *am* a psychologist.

CATHY: He's a Jungian.

MARK: Stupid Freud! He doesn't think the id is governed by CUL-TURALLY INHERITED TRAITS!

Greg was an expert straight man. Paul's writing was note-perfect. Cathy's character was hilarious. All I had to do was hold on for the ride. I've been holding on for eighteen years now. I have written more of the show than anyone else in its history and I've been a cast member for longer than anyone besides Cathy Jones. I've even outlasted four prime ministers. I had big shoes to fill but, unlike my first day, the shoes finally fit.

Little did I know, however, the wear and tear those shoes would take over the next few years. I once thought of Trinity as the end of the world. But it was just the first step away from home. In the coming years, my career would launch me into places I hadn't even dreamt of seeing. I would leave part of me behind and find much more of myself along the way. But none of that would matter unless I found my own voice.

6

THE ROAD

THE FIRST SONG I ever learned to sing was called "Sonny's Dream." When company came over, my parents would put me up on our kitchen counter and I would belt it out like a pint-sized Pavarotti. In Ireland, they claim it as a national folksong, made famous by Christy Moore. The Americans, too, have taken ownership. There they say it's an old country song, made famous by Emmylou Harris. It is, however, a Newfoundland song and it isn't even very old. It was written in the 1970s by Newfoundland's man of a thousand songs, Ron Hynes, and has since become an unofficial anthem for the province.

The song tells the story of a young Newfoundland boy who longs to see the world. In one verse, the lyrics go:

It's a hundred miles to town, Sonny's never been there,
And he goes to the highway and he stands there and stares.

That song felt like it had been written for me. Our little house was miles from anything or anyone. I longed to crawl inside the TV set in our living room and see the exotic places that flickered on the screen— New York, London, Moscow. It didn't matter. Anywhere but where I was. My parents would always dismiss my yearnings, much, I suppose, as they had dismissed their own.

My father knew more about show business than anyone I ever met. He searched the papers for news of the latest Broadway shows, sucking every morsel of knowledge he could from every entertainment feature. But whenever I asked him why he didn't book a trip and take in a show, he'd look at me as if I was mad.

"Good god!" he'd sputter. "What would you want to go to New York for? You'd get mugged," he'd say as if it was a fact. "It's just noise and pollution," he'd say, convincing himself more than me. "Why go see Broadway? You've got everything you need here. There's a hypnotist doing a show next month at the Arts and Culture Centre. You could go see that. Just as good. You're only paying for the name anyway. Broadway. It's just a street. We have perfectly good streets here."

My mother's family had come from Ireland and she lived for all things Irish. She only ever listened to Irish music and only ate Irish cuisine, which meant boiling everything until the colour of the vegetables drained away and had to be skimmed from the top of the pot water. Her Irish grandmother had mostly raised her and she spoke with a rapid-fire lilt that would have her fitting in at any pub in Waterford. She often spoke of how her life's dream was to see the green fields for herself, but whenever I suggested she just buy a ticket and go, she'd turn on me.

"My-god-are-you-cracked? You'd-be-shot-over-there! That-crowd-would-ask-ya-if-you're-Catholic-or-Protestant-and-if-you-answered-wrong-they'd-bomb-ya-where-ya-stood! That's-if-the-plane-didn't-crash! Some-sight-I'd-be-now-bouncing-around-the-ocean-holding-on-to-my-seat-cushion-for-a-floatation-device. Go-to-Ireland? Yes! If-the-IRA-don't-get-ya-the-sharks-will! Are-you-cracked? For-the-love-of-God!"

My parents seemed to have made peace with a belief that the world ended somewhere just beyond their own view. It stopped at the tree line on the horizon. And they tried to convince me, as they had convinced themselves, that the world outside our home was as dangerous as it was boring. But I never stopped dreaming of travel.

Sonny's dreams can't be real, they're just stories he's read
They're just stars in his eyes, they're just dreams in his head
And he's hungry inside for that wild world outside
And I know I can't hold him though I've tried
And I've tried, and I've tried

The truth is, very few Canadians actually get to see their country. It's far too large. The flight from St. John's to Vancouver is longer than the flight from St. John's to London, England. The weather being what it is, most Canadians would opt to visit the crowded beaches of Florida before they'd ever think of seeing the vast and glorious beauty of Nunavut. But each week, as a roving reporter for *22 Minutes*, I found myself hurtling towards some new destination entrusted with a ridiculous and impossible mission.

The road had finally opened up to me. Never having been anywhere before, each new trip seemed wild and exotic. It didn't matter to me if it was to Beijing or Moncton.

I quickly learned that there is nothing like a road piece to give you a rush. These are the segments that viewers most remember from the show because they're exciting to watch. A cast member accosts a politician or celebrity, usually at a press event they weren't invited to, and tries to keep from getting evicted long enough to deliver a few jokes. It's sort of like riding a bull, except in a rodeo, you only have to hold on for eight seconds and the bull doesn't have security guards trying to pull you off it.

The *22 Minutes* producers might come in and tell you, "The prime minister is giving a speech in Ottawa tomorrow. We want you to fly there and ambush him." Then, handed this impossible task, you find yourself on a plane with a notepad in your lap, furiously writing down gag ideas that you will undoubtedly forget the moment you find yourself in the thick of it staring into the PM's eyes.

People often ask me if the ambushes I do are set up. The answer is no. An ambush involves hours of stakeouts, usually in a parked car or a hotel lobby. The chase is exhilarating. You lie about credentials. You run away from security. You hide behind pillars. The camera operator and producer mingle with the other press at the event, trying to get a lead on which door our target is going to being entering and leaving from. Meanwhile, you'll wander around with a microphone jammed into your suit pocket, trying to fit in. Then, when your intended victim shows their head, you pop out and try to keep up as they scurry away, peppering them with as many questions as you can get out in the minute or so until they escape into their car or elevator or office. It's easily an hour or two of waiting for every minute of film that makes it to air. You can prepare yourself for any number of outcomes but you never know what will happen.

As it turns out, it's in those moments, when everything goes out the window and there is no net to catch you, that I thrive. But it wasn't always that way. That confidence had to be earned.

~

The first politician I ever ambushed was Mike Harris, former premier of Ontario. Mary Walsh had previously ambushed him in 1997 as her Marg, Princess Warrior character. Mary marched into the foyer of the Ontario Legislative Building waving a plastic sword and threatening to "smite" the premier. It had been one of the show's most iconic moments.

The show's producers had heard that Harris was speaking at a hotel in downtown Halifax and thought it would be a great idea to send me down there to "get him." The only problem was that I was twenty-eight, very green and I didn't know much about Mr. Harris at all. My producer told me not to worry about it. "Just do what Mary does. March up to him, grab him by the arm and get a monologue out before he can speak." For someone who had never told a joke professionally in his life, it might have seemed that easy. But I knew better. I made the short drive to the hotel in silence, wondering what I was going to say.

I waited in the corner of the hotel lobby, ready to pounce as soon as Harris stepped off an elevator. Harris was testing the waters to possibly come forward as a political saviour for the Canadian right. The right was split between two parties at the time—the Progressive Conservatives and the Canadian Alliance. A merger of the two had been announced and Harris was being floated as the perfect man to "unite the right."

Nobody took any notice of me. Why would they? I hesitated as I looked around the room filled with Harris supporters. What was I doing? I was easily the youngest person in the room. Who was I to tell this guy off? Maybe, I thought to myself, if I just let him walk past, then I can say he got away and I can go home. Cameraman Pete Sutherland fired up the light atop his camera and nudged me forward with a little the-best-way-to-learn-how-to-swim-is-to-be-pushed-off-the-wharf kind of tough love.

I stepped in front of the former premier and grabbed his arm as I launched into my monologue. Harris barely even registered my presence. He kept moving forward as the flashbulbs belonging to the other reporters' cameras popped around us. Then Harris cut me off and asked, "Where's Mary Walsh?"

Some of the people in his entourage began to laugh, but not at anything I had said, just at me in general. The tables had turned and I was the one getting roasted. I struggled to get my footing like a newborn calf. I managed to get a few lines out, but the room began to spin for me as I realized that I was failing miserably. Harris walked off with a smile on his face, and I limped back to the studio with egg on mine.

It was a great lesson to learn early on. If I was going to succeed, I couldn't imitate someone else. I was going to have to find my own way.

~

That same year, Sherrie and I were blessed with the birth of our second son, Will. He came to us in September, just as the *22 Minutes* season was starting, and for the first time in months, I didn't think of the show.

I paced around the hospital room in the way that expectant fathers do, faced with the sudden realization that despite all of those breathing classes, I really wasn't of much use. I sometimes think that the tasks they teach dads in those pregnancy classes are less about preparing us to help the moms during childbirth and more to keep us out of the way when the time comes.

This being my second child, I was an old hand when it came to being useless. I knew that my only real job was to track down the anesthesiologist so Sherrie could get an epidural as soon as possible. Being a good dad during childbirth is akin to being a good host at a house party.

"Can I get you anything?" you ask the mother. "Ice chips? Another pillow? Needle injected into your spinal cord in between contractions?"

I stood there, shouting out my support like a sports fan watching the game from his couch. Nothing I was saying was going to change anything but it made me feel like I was a part of the team. "Push! Hurry! Hurry, hard!"

Sherrie braced, pushed, and miraculously, another human was in the world. "It's a boy!" I shouted, not wanting to be scooped. But something on the faces of the hospital staff made me more worried than I had ever been in my life—and I'm a Catholic. The doctors took our son to the far corner of the room and the nurses gathered around him in a way that felt to me like an impenetrable wall.

"Is he okay?" Sherrie asked. "Why isn't he crying yet? Can I hold him?"

"Can Dad come over?" the doctor asked, and something in her voice made the air feel thick. The short walk from Sherrie's bed to the doctor's huddle must have been no more than five feet but it felt like it would take the rest of my life.

I looked down at my son, perplexed. He was as cute as could be. His head was covered in thin white hair that looked like a dandelion that had gone to seed. But when he finally made his first cry, announcing himself to the world, I could see much of his top lip and the hard palate of his mouth were missing. His cute little face looked like a puzzle that was missing a piece.

He had been born with cleft lip and palate. We could not have loved him more. When Jacob, just five at the time, met his brother for the first time, he kissed him and hugged him and didn't even notice the cleft. The world would be a much better place if everyone was five.

Over the next few years Will would endure a litany of doctors' appointments and operations without ever once complaining. Today, Will Francis Critch has the nicest smile I've ever seen. Each time he smiles I'm reminded of all that he has overcome.

Working on *22 Minutes* still meant that I was often on the move, and Sherrie had to juggle more than her fair share of busy days and sleepless nights. Will needed a special bottle. He had a dental plate to close his palate that needed to be held in place with an adhesive. Plus she had another young son to raise as well. And she had to deal with it all alone for weeks at a time while I was a province away, making faces in wigs.

I tried to compensate by being on deck full-time when we weren't shooting, but you can never make up for the time you miss. I remember more than one late-night phone call from Sherrie, exhausted with a crying baby in her arms. I probably missed as many calls as I remember. When I reflect on my time on the road, the memories are bittersweet.

I knew the cost of being away from home was high. I vowed that if my work meant I was going to miss even more time from my family, I would give it my all.

~

Following the Harris ambush, I felt as though I was in over my head when I was sent back out on the road. I didn't know the players as well as I should. I didn't comprehend the context of what was happening. How could I satirize something that I didn't have a strong opinion of?

Luckily for me, I had come to cover Canadian politics during a time of great change. It soon wouldn't matter anymore if I knew who was who. Old party leaders were being pushed out, new candidates were fighting to take their place, and entire parties were imploding. Most folks would think that Canadian politics are boring. In 2003, Canadian politics was practically Shakespearean.

The right and the left were fighting more with themselves than with each other. The Progressive Conservative Party and the Canadian

Alliance were splitting the conservative vote. Future prime minister Stephen Harper was leader of the Canadian Alliance, and the new party was drawing Progressive Conservatives who felt their party wasn't regressive enough. The PC's dashing new leader, Peter MacKay, had won the leadership by signing an agreement, written on a napkin, not to merge with the Canadian Alliance. But MacKay quietly rolled over and let Harper merge him to death and thus was born the Conservative Party of Canada. How could you not love that? Canadian politics had more drama than *Coronation Street*, although the plot moved at about the same pace.

I heard that a freshly merged Harper and MacKay were appearing at an event together and I showed up to crash the party. Like me, they were up-and-comers. A new generation of politicians meant I found myself on equal footing.

I walked into the ballroom of the event, the glow from Pete's camera light indicating that the show had started. I still felt nervous, but the butterflies were no longer dancing in my throat. They were flying in circles in my belly, threatening me with the possibility of starting my interview by vomiting all over the two MPs, but at least I felt comfortable with opening my mouth this time.

"Now, Stephen," I began, "some people say there is no room for the Tories in the Alliance Party but there is because every couple of weeks one of your members says something nutty and gets kicked out of the party."

Harper feigned a smile for Pete's lens but I could tell he wasn't having any fun. MacKay started to speak, to try to gain control, but I had learned my lesson from Mike Harris: I would be the one cutting someone off this time.

"Well that's amazing," I said, pointing to Harper. "Peter's talking and Harper's lips aren't even moving. It's magical."

"I got you a present, Peter," I said, handing MacKay a large package of napkins. "I know you have a lot of signing to do, so I got you some stationery."

Not wanting Stephen to feel left out, I passed him a roll of toilet paper. "And for Mr. Harper," I continued, "I got you some stationery as well. Some good three-ply. A lot of people are saying that this merger isn't worth the paper it's written on. I say it is." Peter laughed and smiled for the cameras. He wasn't the one holding toilet paper. The future prime minister, however, stared at me stone-faced.

The flashbulbs popped as the photojournalists rushed to get a shot of Harper holding a roll of toilet paper in the middle of a black-tie fundraiser. He tried to give it back to me once the cameras were off, but I insisted he keep it. He was sure to get some use out of it. After all, I figured, he was full of it.

~

The Conservatives were not the only party to nearly self-implode in a power struggle in those days. Chrétien's finance minister, Paul Martin, was attempting to push out the "old man" at the top. The party was crying out for generational change, even if Chrétien was only five years Martin's senior.

Finally, Chrétien agreed to step down so Martin could step up. A party convention was planned. One night of the love-in would be Chrétien's wake and the following evening would be Martin's baby shower. The very same people who had stabbed Chrétien in the back while patting it were going to pull their knives out of his corpse on a Friday and use them to cut Martin's cake on a Saturday. This meant that I was being sent to cover my first Liberal leadership convention. I couldn't believe it as I placed the accreditation lanyard around my neck. I felt like Cinderella. I was going to the ball!

I stood in the back of the room at Chrétien's farewell party feeling disbelief. Canadian superstar Paul Anka was onstage, crooning his way through the song he had written as an anthem for Frank Sinatra. Anka had rewritten "My Way" in tribute to Chrétien in a cheesefest that showed he was as far past his best-before date as the PM he was honouring. My mouth agape, I listened as Anka sang, "The gays all sing your praise, for days and days, though you wouldn't wed one." The crowd roared as I leaned in closer to see if I had heard him correctly. Maybe it was time for a changing of the guard after all.

The Martin years were beginning, and I knew I couldn't return to the studio without interviewing the new PM. But Canada's next prime minister wasn't the real star of the event. Chrétien may have snagged Paul Anka for his big night, but Martin had somehow booked Bono. The U2 front man had agreed to speak at the Liberal convention because of Martin's promise to excuse third world debt. That's one hell of a rider.

Pete and I showed up early to stake out the place and see if we could get close enough to the action to ask Martin and Bono a few questions. A grizzled Mountie with an earpiece blocked our way like a nightclub bouncer waiting for a tip.

"What the hell do you think you're doing?" he asked through squinted eyes that made him look like a hacky impressionist's attempt at Clint Eastwood.

"We're allowed to be here," I said, naively flashing my laminated pass at him, like a radio contest winner backstage at a Trooper concert.

"I know who you are," he said. I was at that strange point in my career where my audience didn't really know my face but the Mounties did. "I don't want any trouble here tonight," he growled in a voice that made him sound like he gargled with broken glass. "We have a very important guest here and I don't want you ruining anything."

"You mean the prime minister?" I asked.

"No," he said, "Bono." Poor Paul Martin.

"Bono?" I repeated innocently. "Like, Cher's ex-husband?"

"You know who I mean!" he shouted. "Now listen to me, shit flows downhill. And I'm on the top of the hill. And you're at the bottom of the hill. Do you understand what I'm trying to say?"

"You have to go to the washroom?" I answered, unable to resist an opening like that. "There's a men's room in the lobby." I mustn't have been looking as intimidated as he had hoped because he moved off. "I'm watching you," he spat back over his shoulder.

"Thanks," I said. "I appreciate you catching the show." Despite my cavalier attitude, I was beginning to think that we might actually be screwed. This guy was on to us like cheese curds on poutine. It was then that Pete noticed a side door that led to the backstage area.

There was just one cop guarding the door and he looked as young and green as I did. The event hadn't even started. He tried to check the credentials of the lighting and sound techs who breezed past him, having long since stopped caring about whoever the act was they were supporting. To them, this was just another gig that needed to be set up.

We concocted a plan. Pete brushed past the guard without stopping.

"Hey! No media. Come back!" the cop shouted after Peter, who by then was long gone down the hallway. Before he could chase after my errant cameraman, I got in his face.

"Hey! Did you just see a guy with a video camera go by here?" I asked. Yes, I was told. One had just run past him.

"Ugh," I moaned. "Stupid cameramen, am I right?" The cop smiled and nodded, as if he always had to deal with crazy guys brushing past him with a camera on their shoulders. "I'll go grab him and bring him back. I need him out here. Thanks." And before he could say anything, I, too, disappeared down the hallway.

"Over here," Pete called to me from behind a stack of gear. We stashed his camera behind some travel cases for lighting equipment. I removed my blazer and tie and rolled up my sleeves. We turned our media passes around and did our best to blend in with the crew.

"They're serving food," Pete said and wandered over to the catering area. He loaded up his plate as calm as a cucumber, sat down next to a lighting guy and within minutes he was deep into a conversation about cables and lighting gels. I sat down in a corner and waited. We must have been there for a couple of hours when there was a great flurry of activity. Bono had arrived. We grabbed our stuff and hurried into the dark area where he was chatting with Canadian rock legend Ron Sexsmith and U2 producer and Grammy winner Daniel Lanois. Anka, Bono, Lanois, Sexsmith? This Liberal convention had a better lineup than the Junos.

We popped out of the darkness, camera rolling. Bono barely flinched as I made a couple of Paul Martin jokes. He listened patiently as I finished my spiel. Then Bono went into his, speaking at length about third world debt, poverty and the ravages of AIDS in Africa.

It is very hard to make jokes about third world debt, poverty and the ravages of AIDS in Africa.

As I felt the humour being sucked from the room and my road piece curling up into a ball and dying an early death, I noticed my grizzled Mountie friend slink into the room. He was followed by the young man Pete and I had blown past. The junior cop pointed at me as if he was picking me out of a police lineup that consisted of me and a couple of pop stars. I had found the bottom of "shit hill."

I doubled down, asking Bono what the folks at home could do about third world debt. I knew they wouldn't interrupt Bono to arrest me while he was waxing poetic about getting pills into the mouths of sick Africans. I also knew I couldn't make any jokes about such a serious topic. I could see my worried face reflected in Bono's wraparound sunglasses. I was sinking in the quicksand of sincerity. More and more guys in trench coats began to fill the room as Bono told Canadians which websites to visit to learn more and donate. Eventually Bono ran out of things to say—perhaps for the first time in his life—and thanked me for my time.

"Anything else?" I asked, desperately.

"No. That's about it," he said, having spoken long enough to get tired of his own award-winning multi-million-dollar singing voice.

I thanked him, turned to the cops and extended my arms. "Gentlemen?"

They grabbed Pete and me, one on each of our arms, and hustled us back the way we had come. "Were we not supposed to be here?" I asked.

"Shut it," the top cop muttered. Luckily, he seemed to want us gone before anyone else realized we had made it past him. We were dragged past a dressing room door with a piece of paper taped to it that said "PMO."

"Is this where you want me to go?" I asked, pointing to the door with a smile. The only answer I received was an icy glare. Some people just don't know how to have fun.

To our surprise, we weren't escorted from the building. We were simply told to "get out of here" as our guides ran back to Bono. We shrugged and mingled with the crowd of Liberal fanatics as we awaited the big moment when Paul Martin's spotlight would be stolen by a rock star on the night he became prime minister in the worst public relations planning in recent memory.

Bono sauntered onto the stage with the swagger of, well, Bono. The Liberals went crazy, beating their inflatable thundersticks and screaming with religious fervour. "Look how cool Paul Martin is! Bono is here! Things will be different now that the old guy is gone and the slightly younger guy who was the old guy's finance minister is in charge!"

"I'm a fan of Canada," Bono brooded in his moody Irish lilt. "I believe the world needs more Canada," he sulked. "Canada—O Canada—will show the world the way forward," he said seductively, sending the Grits into near Pentecostal-level convulsions of piety. From across the room, I locked eyes with the man who had just tossed us from the building. He waved me away from his beloved Bono as if I was a child about to touch a hot oven door. He began to push his way through the crowd towards us, but his way was blocked by row after row of lifelong Liberals having the time of their long, Liberal lives.

The Mountie did his best to hack his way through the party hacks as I made my escape. I approached a group of young Liberals who clearly recognized me only because they were nerds. "Hoist me up?" I asked. "I'm gonna crowd-surf." This was the closest thing to a concert that these young political hopefuls had ever been to, so they happily lifted me up over their heads and began to pass me along. The great thing about crowd-surfing is that it's the perfect way to avoid security. Pete got a great shot of me bobbing over the crowd. This was all going to cut together well. All we needed now was the PM.

Pete and I lay in wait late into the night. We found a hallway that led into the hallway in which Martin would most likely leave after speaking to a group of young Liberals. I stood, hearing the chants of the Martin youth as they filed in behind him. As he approached, Pete and I popped into the hallway and I linked arms with him. The enthusiastic Liberals were so loud behind him that I don't think he even heard a word I said.

"Here he is, the new prime minister! Junior is with me," I began as Martin faked a smile. "It's been all about the generation gap, the kid is here with the Paul Martin Youth. The kids love him. It's a big generation gap. There's a new generation of prime minister, like four years difference or something like that, and he's hopped up on himself, too, like a young person in the back seat on prom night, all horned up, just ready to rip the prom dress off the country and screw it to the boards!"

With that I let him go, and Pete and I ran off down another hallway, full of adrenaline, like kids who had egged their teacher's house on Halloween. We returned to Halifax, where the *22 Minutes* producers were full of questions. Questions like, "What did you do?" and "What were you thinking?" The Prime Minister's Office had called the production office in an uproar. They were furious that I had spoken to Bono and demanded to know what I had said to him. I insisted that I hadn't done anything to upset the Irish Elvis. The tape had all the frivolity of a Sarah McLachlan PSA for homeless dogs.

That didn't matter to the PMO. They said that if any of the Bono footage aired, *22 Minutes* would be banned from Parliament Hill and we would lose all access to anyone in Martin's cabinet. We could use any footage with Chrétien or Martin, fine, but showing the image of Martin's BFF Bono would be tantamount to broadcasting an image of Muhammad.

It was an easy deal to make. Our piece aired, minus Bono but with two prime ministers and a great shot of me crowd-surfing at the Liberal convention. As it turned out, Martin shouldn't have been so protective of his friendship with Bono. The rock star soon started to criticize him for reneging on his promise to raise Canada's foreign aid. "I'm bewildered, really," Bono said in 2005. "I'm disappointed. I can't believe that Paul Martin would want to hold up history." And with that, Bono learned what most regular people already knew—not to trust politicians.

That year was a turning point for both the Liberals and the Conservatives, and it was for me as well. Both parties had new leaders. I, too, had fought to earn my place. In my own small way, like Martin and Harper, I too was starting fresh. It felt as though anything could happen, and I wanted to be there when it did.

7

DAMN YANKEES

HAVE BEEN SPOILED. Canadian politicians are the easiest politicians in the world to get close to. You can walk up to just about any Canadian politician and start filming and they will just stand there like a moose blinded by the headlights. Some even bask in the glow of the spotlight, like a dying flower leaning into the lone ray of sunlight peeking through the blinds of a basement apartment window. They are docile creatures. Like wild animals, they are more afraid of you than you are of them.

In contrast, the first time I tried to speak to an American president, I was almost shot.

George W. Bush Jr. was running for re-election and I was sent to cover the election for *22 Minutes*. I made my way to Florida, arguably the "most shooty" of states. I would be the farthest I had ever roamed in my thirty years on the planet. I remembered how exotic Florida had seemed in my childhood. The rich kids in class would vacation there and sit in class on the first day back from Christmas break with mouse ears on their heads. But this was no Disneyland. Mickey Mouse was nowhere to be seen (though it could be argued that I had been sent to meet Goofy).

As I had done so easily in Canada many times before, I was going to ambush Bush. We were not accredited to cover the event, but we figured we could throw on some Canadian charm and "sorry" our way in.

ME: Oh, hi, eh? Is this the George Bush rally? We're here to cover it.
SECURITY: Are you on the list?
ME: Aw, geez, eh? There's a list? I didn't know there was a list. Ya see, we came all the way from up in Canada, eh, and we just wanted to see what a real live president looked like.
SECURITY: Canada? Well, that's just adorable. Come on in. Hey, Gary! These guys are from Canada! Get a picture of me petting them.

In reality, we had arrived a little late. The president was scheduled to speak inside a stadium in mere minutes, and security was tight. I marched up to the security gate and began the usual drill.

ME: Oh, hey! We're from Canada, eh? Sure is warm here. I hope I get to see my first orange!
SECURITY: Sorry. The event is closed to media now. You should have been here half an hour ago.
ME: Yeah, but we got lost cuz the buildings are so big, eh? And there's no snow so our Huskies can't—

The guard turned and stared off into the distance. Flying overhead were two identical helicopters—one, Marine One, carrying the president, and the other, a decoy. It must be a great job to fly a helicopter whose sole purpose is to be shot down instead of Marine One.

The two helicopters landed just outside of the stadium and out of one popped Bush the younger. I had never seen an American president in the flesh before, and for a moment I was stunned. The guard snapped to attention and I saw my opening. With all eyes on arguably the second-dumbest man to ever hold the office of president (at the time he was the dumbest), I made my way to the metal detector gate and quickly walked around it. My cameraman, Pete Sutherland, followed along instinctively. We were sneaking around like we had many times before in Canada. But we weren't in Kansas anymore. We were in Florida.

I began to speak into the camera as we made for a door that would lead us to Bush. "Florida! Hurricanes, tropical storms and now George W. Bush has landed. Why is God so mad at Florida?"

A motorcycle cop came out of nowhere and roared his way across the parking lot, blocking our path.

"Put it down," he shouted, gesturing towards Pete's camera. Pete slowly lowered his camera to the asphalt and I dropped my mic as if it was a pistol.

"It's okay," I pleaded. "We're from Canada."

"We're from Canada" was a magical phrase that had always brought out a condescending smile in Americans. But on this day, it did me no good. It was as if I was saying "We're from America" in Paris.

The cop shook his head as he checked our passports, relieved to see that we were, in fact, just a couple of hosers. "You need to leave the property."

"Wait a minute," I whined as I watched someone walking behind the president carrying the "football," the black leather bag that carries the nuclear codes. "Who says we have to go?"

"That guy," the cop answered, pointing to the roof where a sniper lay, his rifle pointed in our direction. Another man stood alongside him watching us with binoculars. His left arm was raised in the air, ready to give a signal. Who was I to argue? This was Florida and I was a snowbird blown off course. It was time to spread my tiny wings and fly away.

Although George Bush Jr. eluded us, we did manage to get to the eventual Democratic candidate in the race, Senator John Kerry. He was speaking in Tampa at a huge outdoor event. The big story of the day was the shortage of influenza vaccine in the United States. There was a lot of pressure being put on Canadian firms to sell their doses of vaccine to Americans instead of at home. Americans were heading to Canada to get their shots, and there was some unfounded panic brewing in Canada that our southern neighbours would bully us out of our so-called "socialized medicine," which they claimed to hate so much!

I had some vials made up that looked just like flu vaccine and I kept them in my pocket. We showed up at the Kerry event and were shuffled

Here I am at 18 years old, right around the time my dad was gently nudging me out of the house.

Tristram Clark

Just a year later I was performing in Rising Tide Theatre's production of *Salt-Water Moon* alongside Ruth Lawrence.

Ned Pratt/Rising Tide Theatre

Neil Robbins

Rising Tide Theatre gave me a crash course in acting with performances in theatres but also in open-air settings like fields and pretend ice floes.

Ned Pratt/Rising Tide Theatre

Care of Sheilagh Guy Murphy/Newfoundland Young People's Theatre

In the early days I did a lot of plays that toured schools. In this one, I played a character with AIDS. The cast might be mad at me for my terrible haircut.

Justin Hall

My first time off the island was performing with Paul Edwards in Halifax in 1993. We were so excited we forgot to find a place to stay.

I love performing stand-up, whether at the Halifax ComedyFest or Just For Laughs, but I much prefer the laughs backstage with fellow comics like Ron James and Rick Mercer.

Chris Smith/Pilot Light Productions

Dreams do come true. I got to write a stand-up act for Fozzie Bear when Tim McAuliffe, Dean Jenkinson and I wrote a live show for the Muppets.

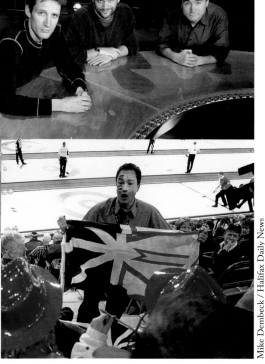

Peter McBain, Kevin White, Paul Mather and I relax at the *22 Minutes* news desk during my first week at the show. Back then there were just four of us in the writers' room. Now, there are upwards of 12.

My first road piece and onscreen appearance for *22 Minutes*. You can take the boy out of Newfoundland . . .

Handing future Prime Minister Stephen Harper a roll of toilet paper. Little did I know that this photo would later get me out of a jam in Jordan.

They say never meet your heroes, but I'm very glad for the time I got to spend with Robin Williams.

The White House Briefing Room. I got to sign my name on the basement wall just one floor below where I am standing.

Trying to make Hillary Clinton laugh so the Secret Service agents don't jump me.

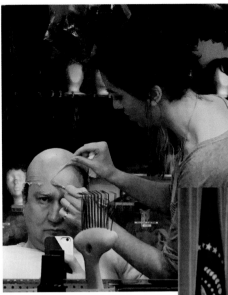

I work with so many talented people who help make my wild ideas a reality every day. Every hour spent in the makeup chair has been worth it.

Of all the characters I've had the chance to play, Donald Trump was the most fun. I never thought that my most bizarre look would be a real person.

My Hipster Chef character became a fan favourite among chefs. I have eaten more than one free meal because of it.

22 Minutes is the longest-running scripted series in Canadian history.

Here I am catching up with some *22 Minutes* alumni backstage at the Canadian Screen Awards.

Shaun Majumder

My trip to Afghanistan to entertain the troops had a lasting effect on me. I admire our troops a great deal. I hope I never have another heckle as bad as being interrupted by a Taliban rocket.

Scotch tastes even better when it's contraband.

When I was a kid, they told us that the Russians wanted to kill us.

Creating political comedy in China
and Jordan is impossible . . . almost.

Getting between the Quaids and Dog the Bounty Hunter made me feel like I was a character in a Bonnie and Clyde movie.

Offering Pamela Anderson a million dollars to stop acting. I'm very glad she didn't cash that cheque.

Michael de Adder

I've found my fair share of trouble over the years. When I interviewed then MP Carolyn Parrish and she stomped on the head of a George W. Bush doll, I thought things would blow over . . . until I opened up the paper to see a Michael de Adder cartoon about a stunt I pulled.

Daniel Murphy

Hanging from the top of the Peace Tower on Parliament Hill gave me the most exciting view I've had in a life of great views.

My friend Allan Hawco and I discovered that our ancestors had been best friends who fought, died and were buried alongside each other in WW1.

There's nothing more exciting than doing an interview without a net, whether with prime ministers like Chrétien or hopeful prime ministers like Scheer or Mulcair.

Lighting joints and boxing with my favourite foil. Prime Minister Trudeau is the gift that keeps on giving.

Canada's former ambassador to the United States, David MacNaughton, hung this shirtless image of me photobombing Prime Minister Trudeau in the gallery at the embassy. You can see the Queen is delighted with the eye candy.

The best parts of filming *The Grand Seduction* were the chats between the takes. I'm forever grateful for the life-long friendships forged there.

My most important role to date has been as dad to Jacob and Will.

The cod moratorium is what first brought me to Trinity. I had to come full circle and pull one from the water on my wedding day, when I caught the best catch of my life.

off to a bleacher in the far back with the rest of the press. You could barely see Kerry from there, and the joke was clearly not going to work from this vantage point.

We approached Kerry's communications person and once again started to do our best Bob and Doug McKenzie act.

"Gee, we're from Canada, eh? We sure would like to show everybody back home how big this place is, eh? Like, could we maybe get a shot from behind the senator, showing the crowd and all that?"

This guy seemed pretty savvy. "No microphones," he said, pointing to my hand-held. "And just the cameraman goes."

"Aw, jeez," I said. "I sure would like to go too. Just to see, ya know, eh?"

His heart must have melted at the sight of these poor, lost snowmen so far from home because he relented. "Follow me," he said with a sigh, and we were ushered past row after row of security guards until we were standing just behind the Democratic nominee for president as he spoke to thousands. But there was no way for me to get to him while he was still on the stage.

"Are you guys finished yet?" the staffer asked, looking at his watch.

"No," we said. "Just need one more shot."

"Well hurry up," he said impatiently. "You're not even supposed to be back here!"

We were running out of time. Pete was trying to stall as best he could. He put the camera on the ground to get a low shot. He put the camera on his shoulder and panned from Kerry to the crowd. He panned from the crowd to Kerry. Had the technology existed at the time, he would have had enough images of John Kerry to print a 3-D model of the man.

"Okay, that's it," the staffer said, finally having had enough. "I'm pulling you out of here." But he didn't have time to take us back to the bleachers with the rest of the media. He needed to be onsite when Kerry got off the stage. He put us in a line with some VIPS who were there to shake the senator's hand.

"Wait here and do not turn that camera back on," he told Pete. And with that he was gone.

This would take some thinking. How was I going to pull the micro-phone from my blazer and not have it look like I was reaching for a gun? I was nervous, but I figured I was fine as long as I kept my cover.

"You the guy from *22 Minutes*?" a man in a hockey jersey asked. Of course he was a Canadian. Kerry had been telling anyone who listened that he had played hockey in high school in a bid to appear more rough-and-tumble. This Canuck was here to present Kerry with a Tampa Bay jersey for a photo op.

"Want me to bring him over to you when I meet him?" he asked. O Canada! I watched as John Kerry walked down from the stage to thunderous applause. He was presented with the jersey as the cameras flashed. Then the man pointed at me, saying, "This guy is from Canada. Can you come over and say hi to him?" I waved. Kerry waved back. And in no time I found myself face to face with the man I had been chasing all day.

I pulled my microphone from my blazer and Pete fired up his camera.

"If you ever need some flu vaccine," I said, slipping him a couple of vials, "I've got your back!"

Kerry was hustled away, and within seconds the comms guy who had been so sweet and accommodating to the poor, melting Canadians was back, so red and flushed that for a moment I considered offering him some of my Canadian flu vaccine.

"Why—what—who are you?" he asked.

"We're from Canada, eh," I began.

"What did you say to him?" he asked. His eyes were bulging from his head, making him look like a frog in a chokehold.

"I just offered him some Canadian flu vaccine."

"You idiot!" he cried. He now looked to be completely in shock. "Do you know what you did? I brought you here. I could get fired for this!"

"Sorry, eh," I said.

"Go," he told me, rubbing his eyes. "Just go. Go out through our private gate and keep going as fast as you can. Don't speak to anybody. Don't mention me. I'm going to say that I don't know who you are. You never saw me! Do you hear me? You never even met me!"

I tried to apologize one more time but he wasn't interested in my good Canadian manners.

"WHY ARE YOU ASSHOLES STILL HERE?" he barked. "GO! GO! GO!"

Sometimes, whenever I see Tampa play, I think of that guy, and on a quiet night, I can still hear him screaming at me.

~

I love my job at *22 Minutes* and I loved it back then, too. It gave me what I had always wanted—a chance to make a living writing and performing my own work. But at times it could be stifling. It still felt like someone else's show. The original cast had made it famous. When people found out that I was on the show, they would sometimes ask what is was like to work with Rick Mercer, even though he had left the show before I had even joined it.

In my early days, the show was in transition. The audience had come to love the original cast. By 2004, Mary Walsh was appearing less frequently. Rick had gone. Even his replacement, Colin Mochrie, called it quits after just two years. Shaun Majumder, Gavin Crawford and I were all competing for regular slots on the show. In some ways, it was a completely different show than the one audiences had come to love in its first ten years.

By now, in my third year, I was doing triple duty, writing, acting and hitting the road, but while many viewers knew the show, they didn't always know me.

I'd walk down the street and notice someone staring at me. *Oh*, I'd think, allowing the narcissism that bubbles under the skin of all performers to seep through my pores for a moment, *I've just been recognized.*

"Hey," the eagle-eyed fan would say. "Don't I know you?"

"Maybe," I'd reply. "I'm a comedian. Must be that. *22 Minutes*?"

"No, that's not it," they would say, rubbing their chin, deep in thought. "Don't you work at the Tims downtown?"

What would it take to finally get noticed? I wondered. To be honest, I had failed to really make my mark. This was nobody's fault but mine.

I had been playing it safe. I didn't feel that the show was my home yet. I felt more like I was housesitting. I was comfortable there, but not so comfortable that I could put my feet up on the coffee table. What I needed to do, I thought, was put my feet on the coffee table—and maybe even break it.

~

Having successfully evaded me in Florida, George Bush beat Kerry and was re-elected. Not long afterwards, Bush decided to repay the favour of my visit and come to Canada. It was around the time Canada had refused to send troops to fight in the war in Iraq. Tensions were high between us and our neighbours on the other side.

One Liberal MP had become notorious for saying things in the press that many feared would raise tensions even higher. Carolyn Parrish was caught on tape referring to Americans as "warlike bastards." She had also likened the American war effort in Iraq to "a coalition of idiots." I couldn't think of anyone better to interview about Bush than an MP with a broken filter. So we asked her office if we could shoot a piece where we talked about some of the things she had said in the past. The idea was that I would try to get her to say some nice things about Americans to smooth things over. Surprisingly, she agreed, and Pete, producer Adamm Liley and I were off to her office in Mississauga.

One of our writers, *Baroness von Sketch* star Jennifer Whalen, kept a George W. Bush doll on her desk. When you pulled the string in its back, it spoke Bush quotes in his voice. Jen suggested that we take the doll with us to use as a prop. The plan was to use it as a stand-in for Bush. Parrish could practise saying nice things to the doll before she met the real president on his visit to Canada. I would even try to make her kiss it.

Carolyn was more than happy to talk about all the things she had said about our neighbours.

"Were you misunderstood, do you think, when you called Americans 'bastards'?" I asked her.

"No, no, no, no," she said enthusiastically. "I wasn't misunderstood. But what I wasn't doing was calling the Americans that bad name. I was probably directing it at the people in charge of the United States going to war."

"Oh," I said, delighted that she wasn't backing down. "So, like, George Bush would be a bastard?"

"Probably," she answered. It became clear to me that this interview would not help Canada/US relations at all. But a sitting MP calling George Bush a bastard on tape ahead of his visit was very good TV.

Despite the vitriol she was spouting, I did get her to give the doll a kiss. By the time we were done with the interview, little George's face was covered in lipstick. All we had left to do was get some B-roll to help with the edit. Most of the cut-away shots involved the doll. Adamm suggested Carolyn could step on the doll if she wanted, and she did. Very enthusiastically.

In the clip, I pass her the doll. She smiles, and drops little George to the floor of her office. The camera zooms in as her black leather boot stomps down hard on his wee little stomach. Then Pete pans back up to get our reactions. Carolyn gives a Cheshire cat grin as I wince. We said our goodbyes, thinking we had a pretty funny little piece—not realizing that a boot was about to land on us as well.

Adamm took the tape to the nearest CBC outlet to feed the footage to Halifax so it could be ingested into the system for the edit. We then headed to the airport and flew home. We arrived back to find the studio in chaos.

"What did you guys do?" the producers asked. I had no idea what they were talking about. "You had her stomp on the president?"

Apparently, some journalists in Ontario had seen the tape being fed through the system. 'Wait," they thought, "is that Carolyn Parrish stomping on a George Bush doll? We must have that tape."

And so the image of Parrish's foot thumping down on an effigy of the president of the United States as if it was a cigarette butt aired on the national news without any context at all. The piece, as we'd intended, would end with her kissing George. Then I'd say, "Peace, everyone," and Carolyn would flash two peace signs. Now CBC Newsworld was going to show the tape before I had even seen it. They had even assembled a panel of pundits to debate its consequence. When veteran CBC anchor Don Newman showed it live on air, it looked less like a joke and more like a violent political statement, and he called the video as if it was a gold-medal Olympic hockey game, his iconic voice adding gravitas to something that was meant to be silly.

"You see her drop the president now," he narrated as if he were Walter Cronkite watching the Zapruder film. "And here comes the boot. We've slowed down the film now. Here the foot comes. And, yes. There's definite contact there. She's squishing it now. What do you say, panel? Is that a stomp? It looks like a stomp to me."

A single boot had not made that much of an impact on Canadian culture since Stomping Tom first sang "The Hockey Song." And then I heard one of the panellists say, "The only thing that could make this worse is if she had stuck needles into the president's head as if it was a voodoo doll!" That was a ridiculous suggestion. I mean, who would do something like that?

Don Newman paused, touching his earpiece. He listened for a moment and said, "I'm being told, now, that she did do just that and we have footage of the stabbing as well."

The news broadcast then cut to me standing next to Parrish at her desk. I put the doll down in front of her and handed her a pen, saying, "Now, if this was a voodoo doll, where would you stab it to do the least damage?" Guilty as charged.

Carolyn then stabbed poor George squarely in his forehead. "No, he wouldn't feel that at all," I say. "Right now Dick Cheney is going, 'What hit me?'" But I was the one who was beginning to get a headache. This was not what I had intended at all. Shown in isolated clips like this, it wasn't funny. It was damning.

I immediately tried calling Parrish's office to apologize, but it was impossible to get through. I was not the only person in Canada who wanted to talk to Carolyn Parrish. I was hoping things would blow over. But that night, CBC's *The National* led with the story.

The show began with the now infamous clip of the boot coming down on poor defenceless George while Peter Mansbridge intoned, "Parrish the thought! Carolyn Parrish damages US relations. How will the prime minister cope?" You know something has become a big news story when the journalists start using puns to describe it.

This was bad. But, I thought, at least this would stay on this side of the border. After all, Americans never pay any attention to Canadian news, right? Wrong. White House spokesperson Sean McCormack was asked about the incident and, in particular, whether the president had any concerns about the criticisms levelled at him by some Liberal members of Parliament.

He answered, "The president and his team have the highest respect for the Canadian people and members of the Canadian Parliament. Freedom of expression is a great tradition in our democracies." At least they had a sense of humour, even if it was missing the *u*.

The next day, the doll incident was on the front page of every newspaper. The *National Post* had a video still of her boot over the doll with the headline: "Carolyn Parrish Should Get the Boot from Caucus for Bush Stomp: Tories." The *Globe and Mail* ran large photos of Parrish and Paul Martin alongside an image of her foot atop the president. Their headline read: "PM Puts His Foot Down—Martin Decries MP's 'Unacceptable' Antics."

That piece, by Ottawa bureau chief Brian Laghi, described how Carolyn Parrish attempted to warn the prime minister about the clip. While Parrish reassured Paul Martin that she wouldn't heckle George W. Bush during his upcoming visit to Canada and gave him a heads up about the spot we had filmed for *22 Minutes*, she left out some of the details. As Laghi wrote, "What Ms. Parrish apparently didn't tell the PM during that meeting was that the video showed her stamping on a doll of Mr. Bush, an omission that Mr. Martin did not appreciate when he turned on the television news at 10 p.m."

So I wasn't the only one surprised by the news that day.

Sensing her time was up, Parrish then gave an interview with the Canadian Press in which she said she wouldn't "shed a tear" if Martin lost the next election. "If he wants to know why he can't control me, I have absolutely no loyalty to this team. None." The next day, Prime Minister Martin met with his caucus and they debated what should be done with the outspoken member. Martin decided that he had to ask her to leave caucus. He stood on a desk in a lobby outside the House of Commons and told members that Carolyn was let go due to the "chronic disrespect" that was shown. The meeting ended with a round of applause.

I finally managed to get in touch with Carolyn and apologized profusely. I stressed that it was never my intent to detonate her career. She bore no malice, and we even shot another interview with her while she sat as an independent MP. We made sure not to feed that tape anywhere, though. As a token of my appreciation, I gave her the Bush doll, which, she tells me, her grandchildren enjoyed playing with. I wonder if the Bush quotes the doll utters when they pull its string will create an impression on them. Maybe they'll grow up on the far-right side of the political spectrum. I doubt she would be as forgiving then.

While Carolyn's star was fading because of that interview, mine was rising. The *Toronto Sun*'s Bill Brioux said, "Mark Critch is making a name for himself on *This Hour Has 22 Minutes*. Critch—rapidly becoming *22 Minutes*' latest go-to guy—sweet-talked his way into Parrish's office and got the Yankee-bashing Parliamentarian to stomp all over a George W. Bush doll. The stunt brought a welcome degree of danger back to *22 Minutes*." He later says, "Critch seems poised to be the next Mercer."

I had finally done it. People were beginning to know me by my own name, even if they still mentioned Rick when they used it. I knew this because when I called home to tell my dad that I was coming home for Christmas in a couple of weeks, he warned me, "They know who you are now!" "Good god," he'd say over the phone as he paced around his kitchen. "You're going to end up on a CSIS watch list. Or worse.

You can't piss off the Yanks. This line could be tapped for all I know. Actually, you know what? I've got to go!"

Click.

~

The new year came, and with it came a new sense of confidence in my approach. *22 Minutes* was known for its ambushes of politicians, but in 2005 we pitched a different kind of road trip. Our prey would be a little glitzier than the finance minister or the premier of Saskatchewan. It would be rich, famous and, once again, American—except this time, it was coming to us.

I was off to Banff, Alberta, for Robert F. Kennedy Jr.'s Waterkeeper Alliance environmental fundraiser. Kennedy used Alberta's world-class ski hills to attract A-list celebrities to help him raise money and awareness for his charity. I, on the other hand, would use it to make fun of those celebrities.

The event was centred around a celebrity downhill ski race. I patiently waited at the bottom of the hill as frozen celebrity after frozen celebrity drifted towards me. I tucked in behind a crew from *Entertainment Tonight*. Once the stars were done being adulated, they naturally walked over to my camera, expecting more praise to warm themselves with.

The only problem was that I often had no idea who I was speaking to until the last possible moment before we rolled. It was minus thirty Celsius with wind chill and the celebs were covered in helmets, goggles and scarves to protect them from the Canadian winter. It wasn't until they were a few feet away from me and removed their gear that I could see who I was about to mock.

I suddenly found myself face to face with Apollo astronaut Buzz Aldrin. This was not a situation I'd ever expected to find myself in. "Hey, Buzz," I said, slapping him on the back as if we were long-lost pals, "you're such a nice guy. Why bother? If I were you I'd be the biggest jerk in the world. If I couldn't get a table at a restaurant I'd pull the waiter outside and point up at the moon. I'd say, "'You can't make me wait for a table! You see that? I've been there!'"

Buzz started to answer, then paused and stared into my eyes with the intensity of a man who was confident he could knock me on my ass despite being seventy-five years old.

"Hey," he said, grabbing my arm, "are you trying to Ali G me?" referring to Sacha Baron Cohen's pre-Borat character. Earlier that year I had cowered in front of the former premier of Ontario. Now, I was happily pissing off the second man to ever walk on the moon. I was finding my groove.

As host of the event, Kennedy basked in the warm glow of the *Entertainment Tonight* camera, waxing on about the importance of a pristine environment, having just flown celebrities in on private jets.

"A quick word for Canadian TV?" I asked humbly as my knees knocked together both from my nerves and from the cold. Kennedy shuffled towards me on his skis, and I was soon hearing the famous Kennedy drawl for myself.

"Everybody knows about the great Kennedy dynasty," I began. "Your father, your uncles Teddy and JFK, but do you ever feel threatened by the great Canadian political dynasties like Ben Mulroney and Justin Trudeau?" This was long before Justin had entered into either the political ring—or the boxing ring—and the idea of him holding high office was still laughable.

"What the hell kind of show is this, anyway?" Kennedy asked, frustrated by my lack of respect for the children of respected politicians.

"It's like the news but drunk," I answered as honestly as I could.

I was in my element, carefully walking the line between charming and annoying. I knew who these people were and I knew how to make fun of them. It was easy. *Seinfeld*'s Julia Louis-Dreyfus, *MacGyver*'s Richard Dean Anderson, *Chicago*'s Catherine Zeta-Jones and other people famous enough to have three names all stopped, smiled, winced and skied away. I couldn't believe my luck.

We wandered the ski hill, looking for more big game on our snowy safari. Then I locked eyes with the biggest game of all. A small man, dressed head to toe in a camouflage snowsuit. If he had been deep in the woods, I would never have seen him. But a camouflage snowsuit makes you stand out on a snow-white ski hill about as much as a polar bear would stand out in a city park. It was Robin Williams.

As a child, I had practically worn out his *Night at the Met* stand-up album. Much of the material was meant for older ears, but I memorized even the jokes I was too young to understand. To me, Robin Williams was bigger than life. Earlier that week I had stood in awe of the beauty of the Rocky Mountains as I saw them for the first time. Now I rubbed my eyes again, to take in the equally stunning sight of my childhood hero carrying a snowboard as he walked straight for me.

I knew enough about Robin Williams to know that there was no "getting" him. He was a spinning top. You simply had to press down once and let him go. I pointed at the snowy hill in front of us and said, "Back in the eighties, this would have been a whole different kind of white powder," referring to his infamous cocaine problem. I immediately winced. Who starts a conversation with a stranger by bringing up their drug addiction? I needn't have worried.

"Yes," he said, his eyes twinkling, "there would be no white left on the mountain." He launched into a Jean Chrétien impression, advising the recently retired prime minister to "go back to Shawinigan; you can hit people like you did before." We went on like that: I'd make a joke, and he would use it to launch into a mind-bending improvisation. Then he'd look back to me, like a puppy waiting for me to throw the stick again.

When I was six, Santa brought me a Mork from Ork doll from Robin's breakthrough late-seventies sitcom. When you pulled a string in the doll's back, it would speak in Williams's unmistakable voice. Now I was pulling his strings in real life and he couldn't stop talking.

As we traded lines, dozens of skiers started to roam towards us. Folks in puffy snowsuits waddled closer like penguins. By the time we were done the interview, a large crowd had formed. Robin had planned to go snowboarding, but now he was trapped.

"I'm sorry," I said sheepishly. "I think I blew your cover."

"Aw, that's okay," he smiled, kneeling next to a little girl who had been standing with her arms outstretched.

"Are you Mrs. Doubtfire?" she asked suspiciously.

"Hi. I'm Robin," he said, kneeling in the snow to meet her eyes. "What's your name?" He was still there after we had packed up, calmly giving everyone who asked for it a little moment with his genius. I was grateful for mine.

~

There is something intoxicating about our southern neighbours. We lean in and pay attention to every little squabble as if they were a couple arguing at the next table on Valentine's Day. They are fascinating. It's hard not to be impressed. Everything there is bigger, bolder and brasher. That doesn't necessarily mean better, though. I wasn't interested in trying to make it in the States.

We have our own stories to tell here in Canada. It just so happens that some of my favourite stories have been about the States. Like Jack, I have tales of giants and golden eggs, but I prefer to tell them after I have made it safely home, back down the beanstalk.

8

BOB HOPE-LESS

FOR SEVERAL YEARS, I have been the host of the Halifax Comedy Festival sponsored by the CBC. Comics from around the country and beyond descend on Halifax for a laugh-packed week of dozens of shows at several different venues. I both love and hate the challenge of coming up with a new stand-up set each year. There is a lot of muttering to myself as I pace in my hotel room, trying to order my thoughts while asking myself why on earth I would ever put myself into this situation, and vowing to never do it again.

The only time I'm not nervous is when I'm onstage. Then something else takes over and for a few minutes I'm lost in the spotlight and the familiar sounds of the crowd. I walk off thinking, "I can't wait to do this again next year!," my brain having erased the worries of a few hours before in an act of self-preservation.

In 2006, I found myself in Casino Nova Scotia between Comedy Fest shows. I was rewarding myself with a drink in the corner, nursing an adrenaline hangover from the success of the first show and just starting to panic about the next one. I was deep in thought and surrounded by the cacophony of bells and whistles from the gambling machines around me.

I felt a presence at my table and looked up to see a young man. He was thin, with a thick forest of jet-black hair and a face that looked like hamburger meat that had been forgotten for a week in the August sun. If you had told me that he stuck his head directly up a beehive on a dare, I would have believed you.

"What happened to you?" I asked without even being introduced. "I mean, hi. I'm Mark," I said, attempting to recover like a figure skater finishing an Olympic routine with a snapped Achilles tendon. "Sorry. You startled me."

"Ithhh okay," he mumbled. It seemed there was something wrong with his mouth. Perhaps his tongue was swollen or his jaw was wired shut. "Mind ifhh I thit down?"

Yes, I minded! Couldn't he see I was working? I was desperately trying to write something, anything, on a cocktail napkin before I took to the stage to try to get laughs out of a room full of people who had most likely just lost their next mortgage payment on a *Beverly Hillbillies*–themed slot machine. The water ring from my drink had soaked my improvised stationery and now the words that I once thought hilarious were all blending into one another like blobs in a Rorschach test.

"Not at all," I said. "Can I get you a drink?" He ordered a beer and I translated for him, declining the waiter's offer of a refill. I had a show to do and I knew not to say "hit me" at this particular casino table too often. I knew when to fold 'em and when to hold 'em.

"So," I said, dispensing with the formalities, "what happened to your face?" I couldn't tell if he was taken aback by my forwardness. It was hard to read his eyes because they were swollen shut.

"I lotht a fwight," he said and with a bent finger he pointed to a poster on the wall. "Ultimate Fighting Tonight" the poster read, "$1000 top prize." Brilliant. I was being rude to a cage fighter.

He slowly explained that there had been a charity match that night. Some amateur fighters were on the bill, too. "I always wanted to be a mickthed marthal awtytht." His words left his swollen, inflamed lips carried not on the air but on a steady spray of pink spittle that ended up on my chin. I dabbed my face with my napkin, forever destroying whatever remained of my once promising routine.

"Youuf got thome ink on your fathe," he said, washing away the stain with spittle from his latest volley of words. The joke was, literally, on me.

"I'm not thuppothed to be here," he added, refilling his reservoir with a mouthful of beer. "I'm thuppothed to be on bathe." Apparently he was in the Canadian Armed Forces. He had asked for permission to leave his base to try his hand in the ring, but his base commander wouldn't give it to him.

"He thaid that iffth I wanted to go, I could go, but iffth I got too hurt to deploy he would have to thay I lefthh withowt permithion." This guy wanted to fight so badly that he was willing to risk his military career to give it a shot. And it appeared he had taken more shots than he had given. He would be going back a loser, but at least he would be going back.

"I'm going to Afghanithtan thoon," he said. This young man dreamt of fighting for a living, but I'm sure he was not looking forward to this next fight. In 2006, Canada was deep into the Afghan conflict. Not all of our young men and women made it back. I waved to our waiter. "Hit me," I said, ordering another. I hoped that my drinking companion realized my request wasn't directed towards him.

I asked him if he wanted to come to the show that night, but he told me that he was already pushing his luck and he had to start making his way back. "Hey," he said as he stood, "you thood do a thow in Afghanithtan."

He told me they had shows on the base in Kandahar from time to time, but the servicemen and women always said they'd love to see more acts from home there. I told him that I'd see what I could do.

My friend Geoff D'Eon was gung-ho right from the start. He had been a 22 *Minutes* producer and now oversaw the Halifax Comedy Fest for CBC. He spoke to a contact at the Department of Defence, then with CBC, and soon we weren't just going to perform on the base, we were going to tape a special there just two weeks before Christmas.

Shaun Majumder came on as a headliner and we added Canadian comedians Erica Sigurdson, Tim Nutt and the late great Irwin Barker to the bill. Before long, we found ourselves flying, along with our crew, straight into a war zone, Bob Hope style.

We flew commercial to Dubai and then, we were told, we would be flying in a military Hercules aircraft to Afghanistan. But when we stepped off the plane, we were hustled onto a bus. Then, as is often the case when the military is involved, someone started shouting.

A man at the front of the bus stood up to address us. "Attention, please! My name is [REDACTED] and I want to inform you that what I am about to say is protected under the Security of Information Act! What I am about to tell you is classified and you cannot speak about this to anyone, including your family!"

I had not signed up for this. The problem with top secret stuff is that you never find out that what you are doing is top secret until it's too late to agree to the top secret thing. I looked around for the string to pull that would tell the bus driver that I wanted to get off the bus, but sadly this bus was only going to stop once.

I am not spilling state secrets here. All of this has been declassified over the ensuing years, but at that moment in time, I was learning things you should never tell a comedian.

"We are taking you to Camp Mirage!" the shouter shouted. *Camp Mirage? Sounds fun*, I thought. *Kind of a Club Med vibe.* "Camp Mirage is a top secret military installation!" the bellower bellowed. We were going to a secret base? I had only ever been to one secret base in my life. It was a treehouse and I was ten. This secret airbase in the United Arab Emirates was being used as a logistics hub for our troops in Afghanistan.

"Camp Mirage is crucial to the Canadian war effort!" the yeller yelled. "It enables us to fly into Afghanistan and drop supplies much quicker! We are here at the pleasure of the United Arab Emirates and there are rules! That is one of the reasons we told you not to bring any alcohol! A group of Dutch soldiers brought some beer into Mirage and the entire Dutch force had to leave the base within twenty-four hours! We don't want you doing anything stupid that would endanger the Canadian war effort in a similar way!"

They had indeed told us that Kandahar Airfield was a dry base and that alcohol was forbidden. I, however, had taken that as more of a suggestion than an order, and at that very moment, as I hurtled down a dusty road to Camp Mirage, I was carrying two bottles of twelve-year-old Oban Scotch in my bag. I had been nervous about fitting in. I'd never really been to camp before. What if the other kids didn't like me? So, I thought, I'd make some friends with the greatest social lubricant since booze—more booze.

I looked over at Geoff and tried to mime that I had two bottles of Oban wrapped up in my underwear. I had taken a mime class once, but I had not yet mastered that particular face and instead looked like I really, really had to go to the washroom.

"There'll be a toilet there," he said with a wink. Hmmm. Maybe I could just flush the booze? But a secret base must be on a septic tank. Would I simply be debasing the base itself?

"We're here!" the crier cried. A big, ominous gate stood like a monolith in the night, and I could pick out armed guards silhouetted against the sweeping spotlights. I thought about telling the loud man that I was carrying contraband, but I did not because I am a coward. If he yelled that much just introducing himself, I could only imagine how he would react when I told him about the booze.

No one will ever know, I thought. *I'll just leave it in the bag and nobody will be the wiser.*

"Place your bags in a row so they can be searched!" the screamer screamed. I immediately pictured Peter Mansbridge hosting the TV news in Canada that night. "Canadian Forces bid bye-bye to Dubai," he'd say, dripping with gravitas. "Canada has lost a crucial advantage in the Afghan conflict because Mark Critch can't go a week without getting pissed."

The bags and TV gear were all laid out in three rows as big, furry, toothy dogs sniffed up and down the line. The servicemen opened bags at random, checking every third bag. I closed my eyes and waited for the inevitable.

"All clear," came the call, and we were waved through. I immediately went from regretting bringing the Scotch to regretting not bringing another bottle. Nothing tastes as sweet as contraband liquor.

Back when I was in Trinity, Dennis, Doug, Rod and I crashed a wedding at Rocky's pub. Dennis checked to see what colour the drink tickets were and then went to the only place in town that sold them. He bought a wheel of each and we drank like kings all night before falling asleep on the bar, our pockets still stuffed with the evidence. We were easily apprehended. This time, at least I had done a better job of covering my tracks.

We were all assigned a bunk and told that we did not have long to sleep because we would be flying out at dawn. That meant I probably didn't have any time to sleep. I still had to get drunk enough to pass out!

My bunkmate, a cameraman by the name of [REDACTED], was checking his gear on his cot. "Hey [REDACTED]," I said, "I need a hand with something."

His eyes grew wide as I showed him a bottle of my contraband booze. They grew even wider as I showed him the second one.

"What the [EXPLETIVE] are you thinking bringing that [EXPLETIVE] here," [REDACTED] said. "Dump it!"

"I can't just pour it out on the ground," I said. "It'd be sacrilegious or something. And I can't just stash the bottles somewhere. I don't want anyone else taking the blame. We're going to have to do the right thing," I said grimly. "We are going to have to drink them."

"We?" [REDACTED] said. "I'm not drinking that. We have to be up at five. You're on your own."

"Wow," I said, shaking my head. "This is war, and I don't know much about war, but I do know that you never leave a man behind in wartime." This was stretching it but I knew that [REDACTED] was a good man, with a rubber arm, that I could twist. I also knew that the best way to block the pain of a twisted arm was by drinking free alcohol.

He stared at the bottles and considered his options. "We're going to need reinforcements," he said.

I crossed the small corridor to the room across the hall and gently tapped on the door. Our other cameraman, [CLASSIFIED], answered the door, rubbing his eyes and yawning like a toddler looking for Santa. He was wearing the kind of faded briefs worn only by men who had been married for a very long time. The elastic had, like the people in the marriage, long since given up on trying to hold anything together. I told [CLASSIFIED] about my biggest worry.

"Can you pull up your underwear a little?" I asked. Then I told him about my second-biggest worry. "I accidentally smuggled two bottles of Scotch onto this secret base and now I have to destroy the evidence."

"Okay, cool," he said with a yawn. "Come in." I had come to the right room. [CLASSIFIED] had never turned down a free drink. He shuffled his way onto his bunk, his private parts swaying back and forth like a drunk elephant's trunk. I would *need* a good drink after seeing this, I thought. The three of us huddled together, like prisoners in *The Great Escape*.

"We're going to need glasses," [REDACTED] said. I had not expected this. I figured we would just drink from the bottle, but he had other plans. He unclipped a multi-use tool from his belt and began to use the scissors to cut a water bottle in two. He did this again and, with the caps left on, we had four bespoke Scotch glasses. We cracked the first bottle, slowly poured it into our impromptu tumblers and began to get drunk with military precision.

0300 HOURS: One man stands watch as we take our first sips.

0310 HOURS: Second glass poured.

0315 HOURS: Third glass poured; a little over one and a half bottles of contraband yet to be destroyed.

0330 HOURS: [CLASSIFIED] has to pee.

0335 HOURS: The first of us tells the others how much they love them.

0338 HOURS: Second man declares love for "best friends ever." Fourth and fifth glasses poured. Men begin to open up about fear/admiration of their fathers.

0345 HOURS: [CLASSIFIED] has to pee again.

0400 HOURS: Both bottles emptied. Phase one of mission completed.

Once we were all good and drunk, we began to talk about the first thing that drunk people talk about: how *not* drunk they are.

ME: I'm perfectly fine.

[REDACTED]: I wish we had two more bottles. I'm fine.

[CLASSIFIED] *vomits*

[REDACTED]: What are we going to do with the bottles?

[REDACTED] climbs into [CLASSIFIED]'s bunk. [CLASSI-FIED] was already sound asleep, his well-worn briefs stretching from hip to hip like a beauty contest winner's sash.

What *were* we going to do with the bottles? My late-night drinking contest hadn't really accomplished anything at all. Nobody would believe that I had brought two empty Scotch bottles with me. What to do with the evidence?

I looked at my co-workers, sleeping sound, shoulder to foot, as I swayed back and forth in time to their snoring. I pulled the pillow from under [CLASSIFIED]'s head and picked up the tripod he had stored with his camera gear.

I emptied the pillow from its case and replaced it with one of the empty bottles. Lifting his tripod head like a mallet, I proceeded to use it to smash the bottle into pieces. I repeated this process with the second bottle in a flash of drunken stupidity/brilliance.

Just as the POWs in *The Great Escape* had walked around the yard dumping bits of tunnel dirt from their pant legs, I would go and dump bits of broken glass in the garbage cans around Camp Mirage.

I left the safety of our sleeping quarters, bouncing from wall to wall in the hallway. My tired, drunken body was impervious to harm as every joint had been well lubricated. The shards of broken glass in my pillowcase jingle-jangled with every step. I looked like one of those teenagers who still go trick-or-treating even though they are much too old for it. Too cool to wear a costume, too broke to pass up free candy, they shrug incredulously at the stunned homeowners as they mumble a blasé, "Trick or treat . . . or whatever."

I ran from building to building, zigzagging through the darkness to avoid the searchlights that were shining only in my imagination. I lifted the pillowcase as casually as I could, surprising myself with just how loud smashed glass sounds when it's dumped into a metal garbage can at four in the morning.

I ran as fast as I could for cover, tripping over my drunken feet and falling to the ground. Luckily, my fall was broken by my bag of broken glass. Two young soldiers passed me. I nodded towards them and they shook their heads at me. They must have wondered who the strange civilian was, out for a walk in the middle of the night with his pillow.

They looked sharp in their tan uniforms. I remember when the Canadian army was first deployed to Afghanistan. We didn't have any sand-coloured uniforms to send them in, having sold off all of ours after the Gulf War. We must have been the first military in the world to have an end-of-summer-season clearance sale. It must have been hard for them to operate dressed like Christmas trees. At the time, I wondered what it would be like if Canadians found Osama bin Laden's hiding place and surrounded him. Osama would stick his head out of his cave, see the army of green on the perimeter and shout back inside, "Hey! Guys! Did somebody put down sod?"

I made my way back to my bunk just in time to turn around again and hitch a ride on a military Hercules aircraft into Kandahar. Picture a 747. Now picture it stripped of every comfort—the seats, that little air knob you turn that feels like an asthmatic kitten is wheezing warm air on your face when you turn it, the drinks cart, the tray table, the overhead compartment that some guy will try and jam a huge bag into that should have been checked, all the while saying, "Strange! It fit in there on my last flight," the screens that freeze right at the good part of the movie for a "Passenger announcement" in both official languages that lasts so long that by the time it is done you've forgotten what movie you were watching. All of those—come to think of it—terrible things are gone. The best way to describe it is that it *looks* like an Air Canada Rouge flight *feels*.

Thankfully, I was still drunk enough to pass out anywhere. I would need all the help I could get on a C-130 Hercules. It is made to take off with a heavy load from a dirt airstrip and para-drop troops and equipment into hostile areas. It's not made for comfort.

Passengers ride on mesh seats, strapped to the inner hull of the plane, facing the centre. There is no drinks cart because there is no room for one. The middle of the aircraft is completely filled with cargo—anything from a pallet of supplies to a jeep—that is occasionally dropped out of the back of the plane as you're flying. There isn't even a washroom—just a hose that hangs behind a frayed curtain. I can't pee when someone is standing at the urinal next to me. I didn't have a chance when there wasn't even a urinal in front of me.

The other passengers were Canadian troops on their way to God knows what in God knows where. They sat shoulder to shoulder in full uniform. Their helmeted heads leaned on their rifles as they tried to catch a moment of rest. I wondered if they were thinking of where they were going or of who they were leaving behind. I wouldn't dare ask.

There wasn't much of a chance of conversation anyway. The inside of a Herc sounds like someone is swinging two lawnmower motors around in a circle over your head by a chain made of running chainsaw blades. The sound is skull-shaking. I have never in my life been so happy to still be drunk because I never would have made it if my hangover had kicked in.

Being friendly, and a little tipsy, I tried to make friends anyway. I turned to the fellow next to me and asked him where he was going when he landed.

He looked at me, rightfully so, like I was an idiot. "WHAT?" He shouted over the sound a paint can shaker makes right before you realize that you need to buy a new paint can shaker.

"WHERE DO YOU HAVE TO GO WHEN WE LAND?"

"I CANT TELL YOU THAT," he shouted directly into my ear. He turned back to face his rifle, leaning his head on the handguard of the barrel. Nobody likes to sit next to someone on a plane that wants to talk. Especially when you're dressed for combat.

I wanted to redeem myself. I wanted to show him that I wasn't just some useless tag-along. I was there to entertain. To do my small part for the war effort. To remind our fighting men and women that people back home cared.

"I'M A COMEDIAN," I shouted, not helping myself. He continued to stare ahead at the giant pile of supplies covered in camouflaged mesh. "I'M HERE TO DO A SHOW ON THE BASE! WILL YOU GET TO SEE IT?"

"NO! I'LL BE AT A FOB."

Oh. I nodded. That makes sense. Cool.

"WHAT'S A FOB?" I howled over the sound of two jackhammers touching drill bits.

He paused to swallow a little of his annoyance and brace himself for what was obviously going to be the worst flight of his life. "A FOB IS A FORWARD OPERATING BASE. PAST THE WIRE."

Oh. That clarified that. I felt like an idiot for asking such a dumb question.

"WHAT WIRE?" I bellowed over a sound louder than the testing floor of a foghorn factory.

At this point his shoulders slumped and he gave in. He turned to me and through a mix of shouting and hand signals he explained that I would be performing at the Kandahar Airfield. I would be far from danger, whereas he was heading directly into it. And, unlike me, this wasn't his first time.

He told me that he had been wounded in an incident a few months back. He ran into the field of fire to try to save his friend and in so doing suffered terrible injuries to his arm. He did his best to protect his friend as he lay, dying, in front of him. The injuries he suffered that day could have been his ticket back to Canada. But he was made of stronger stuff than that. He no longer had the strength in his arm that he had before but he could load and fire his weapon, and he figured that was enough. He couldn't wait to get back out back there and to rejoin the rest of his company. He wanted to make the Taliban pay, not for what they had done to him, but for what they had done, and were still doing, to his friends.

He had finally found a way to shut me up. I sat in silent awe of this man's bravery. My eyes scanned the rows of young men and women in uniform. I had been excited about the trip. I was ready for some adventure. I had been given a helmet. I was flying on a Herc. Maybe I'd even get to hold a gun! I was acting like a tourist in a place where I had no business even being.

It was sobering in more ways than one, and as the alcohol and heat combined to further dehydrate my pale Newfoundland body, I could feel the mother of all headaches coming. I closed my eyes and tried to make myself as small as possible.

"I BUSTED UP MY GOOD HAND BECAUSE OF YOU," the soldier yelled into my ear, with even more gusto than was needed to overcome the roar of the C-130's engines.

"Pardon me?" I asked, unsure that I was hearing him correctly.

"I PUNCHED A HOLE IN MY WALL OVER A JOKE YOU MADE," he hollered. His voice was now loud enough to make the roar of the Allison T56-A-1 engines seem like the purr of a frightened kitten. This man had taught himself how to reload a weapon with his wounded arm and I had made him angry enough to hit something. I started to look around for a parachute.

"I WAS WATCHING YOUR TV SHOW WITH MY WIFE AND YOU MADE A FRIENDLY FIRE JOKE. I WAS SO MAD I PUNCHED A HOLE IN THE WALL," he screeched. His face was getting almost as red as mine.

I searched my muddled mind but what he said made no sense. Could he have mistaken our show for something else? Maybe the *Daily Show* or *Air Farce* or any of the other fake-news shows that were popping up all over the place in 2006 like baby rabbits?

"I THINK YOU HAVE ME CONFUSED WITH SOMEBODY ELSE," I said, knowing full well that I was probably making matters worse.

"NO! DON'T DENY IT! I KNOW WHAT I SAW," he screamed. In today's world, this would be when other passengers started to film us discreetly on their phones so they could upload it to Twitter with hashtags like #PlaneFight and #CancelCritch.

He explained that he'd been home recuperating with his wife and their baby when *22 Minutes* came on and there I was joking about a friendly fire incident. He walked across the room and punched the living room wall with his good hand, putting a small hole in the drywall. What was the point of people dying in Afghanistan when they're joking about it back home?

The more he talked the more adamant I was that I had not made that joke. It's just not something I would write or pick. It was possible that it had been on the show, but I was confident that I hadn't delivered it. Arguing with him wasn't going to help me or help him, though. Looking back, I can't imagine how he must have felt to find himself strapped into a seat next to the asshole who made a joke about his wounded friends.

"I'M SURE IT WAS AT THE EXPENSE OF THE AMERICANS," I said, trying to smooth things over. "NOT THE CANADIANS. IT WAS THE AMERICANS' FAULT. NOT YOURS."

"IT DOESN'T MATTER," he said. "THEY'RE OUR COVER. WE DEPEND ON THEM. WE ARE IN THIS TOGETHER. YOU DON'T GET IT." But I did. Or at least, I was starting to. You could argue that we shouldn't be in Afghanistan. But the fact was that we were. The Canadians fighting the battles didn't ask to be there. They were there because they had to be and they deserved our support.

"I'M SORRY," I said. "IT WON'T HAPPEN AGAIN. YOU HAVE MY WORD."

"FORGET IT," he said as the plane began to descend. "I JUST HAD TO SAY SOMETHING, YOU KNOW? JUST FORGET IT." The plane banked to the side and I slid down the bench, pinning myself closer to him. We had been warned that the plane might have to do some fancy dips and dives to avoid being an easy target as we landed. But nothing could have matched my personal in-air turbulence.

As we grabbed our gear and disembarked, the soldiers headed off together in a loose line towards the briefing area. There was no time wasted here, but they didn't look like they were in any rush to get to where they were going either. I couldn't blame them.

My seatmate, however, made a beeline in the other direction. "Hey," I said, using my normal speaking voice for the first time in ages, "aren't you gonna go to the briefing?"

"No," he said without a look in my direction. "I'm gonna go find my guys." I watched him as he crossed the airfield and disappeared into the waves of heat that rippled up from the tarmac. He had seen enough fighting to last a lifetime and yet he still found something worth fighting for. How? Why?

I realized that I had no idea what was going on in Afghanistan and I didn't think many Canadians really did either. All I knew for sure was that I had flown halfway across the world to cheer up the troops and the first soldier I met couldn't stand my guts. I had a lot to learn.

I took off my helmet. This was no place for tourists.

9

CHRISTMAS IN KANDAHAR

WALKED PAST THE TENTS and temporary structures of Kandahar Airfield to the centre of the base. A large wooden boardwalk encircled a group of trailers to make up a cross between a touring amusement park and a Deadwood-style frontier town.

I was as far away from Canada as you could possibly get and yet there, right in front of me, like a mirage in the desert, stood a hockey rink.

A few soldiers played shinny on the ball-hockey rink, smacking an orange ball across a concrete slab and into the boards. On their days off, Canadian engineers had volunteered to build it and decorate the boards with painted Canadian flags.

A couple of us rushed over to join in the game. Let me tell you something. You have not been checked until you've been smashed into the boards by a member of the Van Doos, the Royal 22nd Regiment of Quebec.

With my face squashed firmly up against the glass, I saw what seemed to be another mirage. There, across from the boardwalk, was a fully functioning Tim Hortons. A Tims next to a hockey rink—they had created a hoser-oasis in Afghanistan.

A lineup of guys in camo stretched out the door. Men with rifles slung over their shoulders waited to receive their daily double-double from Tims workers who looked no different from their Canadian counterparts, except for their camouflage Tims visors. I pulled my face from the rink glass as if I was scraping chewing gum off the underside of a desk and made my way towards the trailer for a coffee. I stood at the end of the line, realizing that I was the only person in line at Tim Hortons without a gun. You don't see that every day. Well, maybe in Alberta?

Canadian soldiers had their priorities straight.

GENERAL: It's go time! Boots on the ground!
PRIVATE: Sir! Yes, sir! Shall we secure the perimeter?
GENERAL: God, no! First things first! Build a rink and open up a Tim Hortons fast before Roll Up the Rim season starts!

The first thing I noticed about Kandahar Airfield was the rink. The second was the Tim Hortons. But the third thing that captured my attention really stayed with me. It was the smell. It was the kind of smell that pushes itself down into your nostrils the way that water from a fire extinguisher would fill your body if the nozzle had somehow become permanently attached to your mouth. It was the kind of smell that will have you desperately attempting to breathe through your ears. This is an odour that was created not by Afghanis but by Americans, Brits and, yes, Canadians. It was the smell of poop. Gallons and gallons of poop baking in the hot Afghan sun.

The smell came from what the soldiers called the "poo-pond," a lake-size giant pool of human waste situated at the edge of the base during my time there. Today, due to a large expansion, it sits smack-dab in the middle.

Nicknamed Emerald Lake, it had a smell that was so strong you could practically see it, the way you can see heat waves rising from Texan asphalt. You often hear people compare things to a cesspool. This was an actual one and it defied comparison. It was the smell of death, diarrhea and teenage feet. When the wind changed it could make even the most war-weary soldier gag. In fact, I wasn't even sure it was the wind. I couldn't help thinking that what I was feeling was not a breeze but the arms of the stink itself, having grown so powerful that it was now self-aware and searching for a new victim.

I was told that a soldier found himself in need of some cash one day, so he made a bet with his fellow soldiers. They pooled their money and bet him $1,000 he couldn't swim from one side of Emerald Lake to the other. He stripped down and made the plunge, like the Michael Phelps of poops. He made it to the other side and collected his money. He also picked up a terrible infection, spent two months in hospital and was eventually sent home.

"Feel that heat," my friend and fellow comic Irwin Barker said, stretching his arms in exultation. I stood next to him, my hand on his shoulder as I did my best impression of a cat trying to hack up a furball. "What's wrong with you?" he asked. The wretched stink of gallons of decaying poop was having no effect on him.

I did my best to ask him how he could withstand Emerald Lake, but every time I opened my mouth to speak, another fecal cloud invaded my senses. "Why—*hack*—no—*gasp*—smell—*uck*?"

"Does something smell bad?" he asked incredulously. "I can't smell anything."

I looked at Irwin in amazement. How could he not smell that?

"I mean, I literally can't smell anything," he explained. "I lost my sense of smell years ago when I had an operation. Does it stink? Is that why my eyes are watering?" Irwin had an incredible advantage. He would have made one hell of a Taliban spy for CSIS.

As I stood there, dry-heaving at the thought, I ran into my "fan" from the plane. I did my best to act as if nothing was wrong, but my watery eyes and the spittle dribbling down my chin showed otherwise.

"Are you—*gah*—are you—*hack*—are you—*HUUUUUHHH*— coming to the show?" I asked. I was thankful that the line at the Kandahar Tims had been so long. If it had been just a little shorter I would have found myself puking up a half-dozen Timbits all over the gentleman's combat boots.

"No," he said, his face softening with pity. "I'm heading out tomorrow. Most of us guys who could actually use a laugh won't be at your show. We'll be out past the wire. Half the people you'll be performing for work at the Tims or the Burger King."

"There's a—*blech*—Burger—*BLARRGGHH*—King?" I asked, wondering how I could be both hungry and vomiting at the same time. He shook his head and started to walk off. I wished him good luck, but he gave me a look that seemed to imply that perhaps I would be the one who would need the luck more.

"Hey!" I shouted after him. "Do you ever—*gack*—do you ever get used—*HURK*—to the smell?"

"Nope," he said, taking a swig of coffee.

I never saw him again, and I've never stopped wondering what happened to him.

~

I lay in my bunk that night but I couldn't sleep. I was missing part of my Christmas vacation to be in Afghanistan. I had been spending too much time away from my kids as it was. I closed my eyes and pictured the kids drinking hot chocolate beside the Christmas tree. But I wasn't the only person far from home. I was lucky enough to be heading home for Christmas Eve, unlike the women and men serving with the armed forces. I shook my head, banishing any visions of sugarplums from dancing in my head.

I got dressed, checking my boots for the giant scorpions we had been warned about back home but which I suspected to be as real as unicorns and Canadian spring. I walked out into the quiet of the Afghan night and spied a grey-haired man in uniform, smoking. He stared off into the night, seemingly unaware that I was there.

"Been here long?" I asked, trying my luck at making friends a second time.

"Just got here," he told me. "We got ambushed."

I was beginning to think that Afghanistan was not a great place for small talk.

"Made a deal with a local warlord. Got complacent. Guy ran up to us. Had a bomb. My buddy didn't have the strap secured on his body armour. Velcro wasn't closed. Got complacent. Didn't make it. Got complacent."

"Complacent." He kept repeating that word over and over, his eyes glazed as he relived that trauma, the scene playing on a loop in his mind. That man would wear that memory much longer than any uniform.

I walked on into the night, trying to clear my head. A little tinsel strung here and there outside of tents and some hand-painted cartoon signs of Santa were the only reminders of the silent nights that people back home were celebrating. I strolled past temporary structures and rows and rows of tents until I came to the latrines and showers. The graffiti on the walls of the toilets were unlike any I had ever seen. The English and French-Canadian soldiers were leaving each other messages in what was like the forerunner of a Facebook wall.

"Vingt-deux's suck" was met with some French words that I didn't understand but could tell were somehow related to penis length. These insults traded back and forth until they ended the way all Canadian arguments eventually end—with either "Habs suck" or "Leafs suck."

I wandered back onto the gravel road and wondered for a moment which was the way back when I heard a hushed voice calling to me. "Hey! You're that comedian, right?"

"That's me," I whispered back into the night, making my way towards the disembodied voice. I eventually made out the shape of a soldier with a towel slung over his shoulder. I hesitated. Was this possibly another person who had a reason to be pissed off at me? Getting told off on a transport plane was one thing, but I didn't fancy the idea of running into a disgruntled soldier in the middle of the dark Afghan night.

"Don't be silly," I told myself. "He's probably just a fan."

"I'm not a fan or anything," he said. "I just wanted to talk to you for a minute."

This was a weird start to the conversation, but I was curious and, more importantly, lost.

"What about?" I asked, subconsciously wincing to prepare for whatever came next.

"Why are we here?"

The question hung in the air like the smell from Emerald Lake. For the first time, I was aware of, and astonished at, just how quiet the airfield was. I could hear the hum of distant generators and the bang of the latrine door, but nothing else. No birds, no chatter. Nothing but the awkward silence between a man with a simple question and another who didn't know how to answer.

"Do you mean 'we' as in you and me or—"

"All of us," he said, a hint of frustration cracking in his voice. "Like, what do they think about us back home? Are people saying we shouldn't be over here? Is it pointless? Is this like a Vietnam type thing? Do people not want us here? What's really going on?"

I didn't know what to tell him. Should I tell him the truth, that I really didn't hear much talk at all about it? No, it wasn't like Vietnam, because at least people had been passionate about Vietnam, one way or the other. When word of yet another ramp ceremony with more flag-draped coffins hit the news, we all paused, briefly bowed our heads, then went about our business. People back home didn't think about it nearly enough. But saying that wouldn't have helped him much.

"Of course they care," I told him. "You guys are making a real difference and we all support you."

"It's okay," he told me, crouching down and leaning against a wall. "I don't know why we're here, either. My friend is a translator. They went into this little town and tried to speak to the elders in the village. Old guy comes out, asks him why the Russians are back. He says, 'We're not Russians. We're Canadians.' Old guy says, 'Yeah? Well I don't know what a Canadian is. All I do know is that the last time a bunch of white guys rolled into my village with guns and jeeps it was the Russians. And they killed my son. So I don't want to talk to you. Keep moving.' The Afghanis don't even know why we're here, man. It's fucked."

He told me that only 16 percent of the population were literate and, of that portion, only 5 percent were women. So they had no way of reading the newspaper or of learning about the world other than what they were told. And the Taliban were very adept at controlling the dialogue in the remote areas of the country. Add to that the fickle allegiances of the ruling warlords and it was very hard to figure out if you were advancing your wheels or spinning them.

I crouched down next to him and struggled to find some words.

"You don't have to say anything," he said. "I just want to get some things off my chest. Some of the guys don't like it when you talk about this kind of stuff. They don't want to hear it. They just want to get the job done. I know I'll never see you again, so I just wanted to talk to someone who'll just forget it and move on."

I'd move on but I knew I wouldn't forget.

"Anyway," he said, suddenly standing, "I better get going. I won't be at your show, but good luck." He slipped into the night and disappeared.

No matter what else happened, I felt that I had, at least, done some good for him by being there. The whole thing felt like a weird dream, but I couldn't have been dreaming. I hadn't slept.

The sky was changing from the black of night to the dark blue of regret—the kind of sky you see when you're coming from the bar too late. Tomorrow was suddenly today, and tonight was show night.

~

That evening, the audience filed in and took their seats in the hall. The stage had been assembled, chairs laid out and a set was made from some camouflage netting and crates. I was reminded of my father, who helped plan shows during World War II at American army bases in Newfoundland and Labrador and Greenland. He met Sinatra, Phil Silvers, Edgar Bergen, Charlie McCarthy (if you can meet a ventriloquist's dummy) and many more. The crowd at this show didn't look much different from the crowds in photos my dad had shown me.

An officer introduced the show and did some housekeeping. Normally, at a regular comedy show, this would consist of "No flash photography and here are the safety exits." This show was a little different.

"In the event of a rocket attack," he began—*Wait*, I thought, *did he just say rocket attack?*—"an alarm will sound. All personnel are then required to leave the room and take shelter in one of the bunkers."

This was old hat to everyone else, but it took me aback. At that point, an alarm sounded. Everyone laughed. It would have been a funny little joke but the alarm didn't stop and that was, well, alarming. I turned around and saw two of the comics, Tim Nutt and Erica Sigurdson, rushing in from outside. Tim is a pussycat, but he looks like a Viking. I couldn't think of anything that would scare Tim Nutt, but his face was as white as me.

"We were out having a smoke," he said, "and I think we just heard a rocket. It hit something."

At this point the officer got back on the mic. "Everyone out, now!" he ordered, and the audience, rather sluggishly, like kids who had been called inside for supper, started to slowly file out of the room.

I was startled at just how calm everyone was. Nobody seemed to be in the least bit worried. I followed them into the night and made my way into one of the concrete bunkers and watched as people started to light up smokes. I turned to the woman next to me and asked, "Could you please tell me why nobody seems at all worried that we are currently in the middle of a Taliban rocket attack?"

"If the alarm goes off that means the rocket hit already," she said bluntly. "This is just in case there's another rocket. There's never another one. Well, almost never."

We waited until we got the all-clear, and the decision was made to carry on with the show. I was the first act on the bill, and I couldn't wait to get started. Suddenly, bombing in front of the audience was the least of my worries. I was much more concerned with actual bombs.

The crowd couldn't have been more welcoming. We had shown we would not be scared off by one measly rocket and we were going to give them the best show we possibly could.

My new material was working well and I had about a minute left when—right in the middle of my final set-up—the rocket alarm went off for a second time. I couldn't believe this was happening. I was being heckled by the Taliban. I glanced towards the man in charge and he gave me the nod. This was no false alarm. I remembered what the woman had told me in the bunker: if the alarm sounds then that means the rocket has already landed. You're safe.

I looked out at the audience. Once again, they didn't seem at all fazed by what was happening. They looked more curious to see how I would react to this situation.

I leaned into the microphone to ensure I'd be heard over the wail of the siren and said, "We'll be right back with more comedy in Kandahar after this missile." The crowd erupted into a roar of approval and we made our way to the bunkers for the second time that night. One of the rockets had almost hit the Tim Hortons. Had it hit, I'm sure the conflict would have raged on for decades.

I watched in awe as our side fired back. I was told that nothing ever happened on this side of the wire, but now I was closer to the action than I'd ever expected to be. One of the soldiers explained it to me this way. He asked me, "Have you ever seen a jeep with a rocket launcher on top? Well, the Taliban don't have the jeep. And they don't have the rocket launcher. But they have the rockets. They get their hands on these Chinese rockets and they go up in the hills and they lean them up in the general direction they want them to go and they fire them into the airfield. They probably got wind of the show tonight so they figure that they have a good shot at hurting a lot of people if they manage to hit the hall the show is in."

Using night-vision goggles, our soldiers peered into the hills around the base. They could see the traces of the heat signature from where the rocket was launched. They fired into that area and it was over. No more rockets. It all seemed like a video game, but it wasn't. Somewhere in those hills, someone had tried to kill us. And somewhere in those hills, that person was now, most likely, dead.

The comics took a quick poll about whether we would continue the show. We were in no less danger onstage than in our bunks, and nobody else seemed in the least bit worried. We'd agreed to do a show in Afghanistan, and this was what doing a show in Afghanistan was like.

I returned to the stage, comically ducking and looking around nervously. "Welcome back to our night of comedy and fireworks," I said. "For those keeping score, that's Taliban two, comics zero."

Most of the words used by comedians to describe their sets are adversarial. They use words like "I killed" and "I bombed." I don't know why that is. Maybe it's the you-versus-the-world feeling you get when you walk out in front of a strange crowd. My friend Irwin Barker used to compare performing in front of a new crowd to coming across a strange dog that you were unsure of. You never knew if an audience was going to bite you or lick you, or in some cases, maybe even hump you.

I would hesitate to say that we "killed" in a war zone, but I was very proud of my fellow comics. The smiles on the faces of the audience said it all. Mission accomplished.

That night I lay in bed trying to process all I'd seen and experienced in the past few days. The rockets and the rink. One soldier who didn't want to talk to me because he hated my guts and another spilling his guts in the Kandahar night because he desperately needed me to listen. Sleep did not come. I watched the sun come up for the third time that week.

I packed my knapsack, checked my boots for the giant scorpions that never came and made my way to the airfield where our ride home was waiting. I was watching our plane being loaded when two soldiers walked up to me to tell me an officer wanted to speak to me.

"I'd love to, guys," I said, motioning towards the Herc, "but I've got a plane to catch."

"You're not going anywhere until you talk to him," they said without a hint of a smile. "We're not asking."

I was ushered aboard a LAV—a light armoured vehicle—and driven to a small office that was far enough from the airstrip to make me very nervous. The soldiers marched me into a small meeting room where a solitary chair sat in front of a wooden desk. My handlers stood by the door as I sat there, wondering what happened if you missed your flight from Kandahar Airfield. Would my bag be removed? Would I get to keep my points?

The door slowly opened and a man entered the room like a newly wound tin soldier. He reminded me of Sir Alec Guinness in *Bridge on the River Kwai.* His greying hair and the crisp khaki uniform that hung on his straight-backed frame signified a man who was used to being listened to.

He sat behind the desk and silently flipped through a folder without giving me a second look. I peered over my shoulders at the bouncers of the worst nightclub on earth. They stared straight ahead, avoiding my gaze. I had the strange feeling that I was about to be interrogated.

"Why are you here, Mr. Critch?" Sir Alec asked me, still peering down at the folder.

"Me?" I stammered like a kid caught looking out the window in math class. *Why was I here? Where was I? How did I get here? How was I getting out of here?* All these thoughts raced through my head, tripping over each other and keeping the answer from reaching my tongue.

"It's a simple question, Mr. Critch," he said, turning a page in his mysterious folder. What the hell was in that thing? Maybe this was just something that happened whenever you flew out of here. Was this customs? Check-out? I needed to breathe. I was paranoid. I couldn't be in trouble. I was just a comedian.

"You're a comedian, aren't you?" he asked.

Oh my god. He could read my mind.

"Do you think there's anything funny about what we're doing here?"

I was starting to get the feeling that this guy didn't watch a lot of CBC comedy Tuesdays.

"Uh, no sir. No. I'm not here to make fun."

"But that's what you do, isn't it? You make fun of people."

"Yes. No. Not like that. I'm just here to do a show for people. Not to make fun of them."

"And what about when you get back to Canada? Are you going to make fun of us when you get back there? Is that the idea? Tell people we shouldn't be over here? That it's a waste of time? That sort of thing?"

Now my paranoia was changing to anger. I had flown half the way around the world at Christmas. I had performed through a rocket attack—*two* rocket attacks. I hadn't slept in three nights. And I had chugged two bottles of Scotch. Admittedly, that last part was my own fault. But I had come for the right reasons. I don't know why this guy was being such a jerk, but I no longer wanted to know what was in his folder. I was a civilian. There was nothing keeping me from leaving and getting on that plane home and I had no problem telling General Patton here just that.

"Look, I have no—"

He turned a page in his folder. "You like to take a drink, Mr. Critch?"

Oh god. He knew about the booze! I was starting to sweat. A lot. So much was now pouring out of my body and down my forehead that my throat had gone completely dry. There was a glass of water on the desk but I dare not reach for it. If pressured, I would deny ever having had anything to drink in my life. I would live my life like a camel.

"Here's the thing, Mr. Critch," he said, his eyes finally leaving the folder and meeting my own. "You get to go home. A lot of people here don't." The greyish-blue of his eyes reminded me of two frozen pools that I desperately wanted to melt and drink. My god, I was thirsty. "I don't know you so I don't trust you," the old charmer continued. "I don't know what you'll say about all this when you get back. It's easy for you to go back to . . ." He looked back down at his folder. "Back to St. John's, Newfoundland. Back to your little green house on Regiment Road."

A dossier! He had a dossier on me! I wasn't paranoid. I wasn't crazy. A wave of relief washed over my body. Or it might have just been sweat. Then, I realized that if I wasn't paranoid, that meant I actually was in a lot of trouble and I immediately started to panic again, but this time with some moral authority.

I wanted to tell him that no matter what it said about me in that creepy folder, I would never make light of what his people were going through. I had come here to do a show but I was leaving with a much deeper understanding of what it meant for the men and women serving here to live with the uncertainty of what tomorrow would bring. Or, for some, an uncertainty of why they were even here in the first place. I wanted to be mad at him, but he was just protecting the men and women who served under him. He was wrong. But nothing I said could change his mind, so why bother?

"I have one more thing to say to you," he said, leaning in to me so that his eyes were level with mine. I felt as though, for a moment, I could see the frozen circles of his eyes begin to thaw and crack. "I'm from Newfoundland and I'm fucking with you."

The two soldiers cracked up laughing. He started to laugh as well, but I failed to comprehend what was happening. The laughter swirled around me like a sandstorm.

"But . . . how did you know where I live?" I stammered.

"My wife and I walk past your house sometimes when I'm home. We do the trail by your place that leads to Signal Hill."

"And the drinking?"

"You were going trash can to trash can in the middle of the night at Camp Mirage. You didn't think someone would notice? You were pretty thorough, though. Good job."

After a few more laughs at my expense, and some talk of home, they all walked me to my plane. My job there was done, but theirs was nowhere near complete. The last eighty-four Canadian soldiers left Afghanistan on March 15, 2014. One hundred and fifty-nine Canadian soldiers died during that mission.

I made it back home in time to spend Christmas Eve with my kids. I was a little more thankful that year as I lay in bed reading to the boys from *The Night Before Christmas*. That night, though, after the toys had all been put together, my mind drifted far away. It wasn't to the North Pole that it took me, but to Afghanistan. As I drifted off to sleep, somewhat guiltily in my own bed, I could still hear that young man in the night asking me, "Why are we here?" I hope he found an answer he could believe in.

10

THE PRICE OF FREE SPEECH

WHEN I WAS A KID, my father gave me a small metal bank in the shape of the globe. I would squint to read the names of the countries that I thought I would never see. Many of the countries that I would trace with my fingers on that dented metal globe are gone now. The lines on a globe are constantly being pulled on and over time they can fray and disappear, like a sweater ruined by a pulled stitch. Czechoslovakia, East and West Germany, the USSR, Yugoslavia. They have all ceased to exist.

A place like the North Pole, which technically isn't owned by anyone, is particularly susceptible to territorial claims. So much so that a geopolitical tug-of-war has been going on at the North Pole for nearly a hundred years now. The fuss is all over a mountain range that I would never have seen on my childhood globe. The coin slot would have covered it.

In 2007, the Russians placed a flag at the North Pole. You would have trouble finding it, however, because they didn't plant it where you would expect to find it. Two MIR deep-submergence vehicles reached the ocean floor under the pole. There they planted the Russian tricolour flag, claiming the pole for Mother Russia in a move straight out of a James Bond movie.

Peter MacKay was the Canadian foreign minister at the time, and his reaction was swift. "This isn't the fifteenth century," he said in a statement. "You can't go around the world and just plant flags and say, 'We're claiming this territory.'"

But in the *22 Minutes* writers' room we thought, *Wait! What if you could?* Someone suggested that I travel to Russia and plant a flag there. Mark Farrell, our showrunner, jumped on the idea. Why not? What could go wrong? And so I was sent to Russia to claim it for Canada.

We needed the flag to be big enough to stand out but small enough to carry without anyone noticing. Our *22 Minutes* art department came up with a great plan. They got the biggest flag they could find and ran a wire through the top to keep it flat in the breeze. They also gave me a telescoping pole on a tripod to use as a flagpole. When the time came, I'd open the tripod, attach the flag to the pole and raise the flag.

We did not have time to apply for a proper visa. If we wanted to enter the country as press we would have had to travel with a government minder, and that would not be much fun. Stephen Harper's communications people were bad enough. I did not want to meet Putin's. So we travelled as tourists. We figured my field producer, Adamm Liley, could film me on the smallest camera we had, and hopefully no one would realize that we were illegally filming a TV show without the proper paperwork.

Just to be on the safe side, we hired a Russian fixer named Ilya to translate for us and to help us navigate Russian culture and avoid being arrested. Ilya had worked with journalists from CNN and the *Wall Street Journal*, but he had never worked with a team that was flying under the radar, and the concept seemed to excite him. Or maybe he was just a KGB agent?

We landed and went straight to our hotel. I was in Moscow. I couldn't believe it. I couldn't wait to visit Red Square. Adamm and I decided to take a stroll and scope out the scene of our stunt. As we left our hotel, we noticed a couple of young Russian soldiers outside. They leaned against a fence and smoked with the dour expression you'd expect after watching decades of depictions in Hollywood action movies. I spotted a few more soldiers across the street walking in our direction and I instinctively averted my gaze as if they somehow knew that I was planning to insult Mother Russia.

We turned a corner and were shocked to see dozens more soldiers lining the street. The closer we got to the square, the more of them there were, like extras casting for a Bond film. Jeeps, tanks and trucks pulling rockets filled the streets. Police cars occupied every parking spot, giving the entire area the air of a Tim Hortons parking lot. Cops and soldiers packed the streets in every direction. I turned to Adamm. "How the hell are we going to pull this thing off?"

We waited to meet Ilya in front of a hotel close to the square. I was beginning to feel self-conscious as I watched the entire Russian army file past. Then we spotted a small man hiding in the shadow of an awning. He wore round wire-framed glasses. A long knit scarf protected him from the cold. He was pretending to be lost in a book but his eyes darted about as if he was searching for some unseen danger. He looked like Harry Potter if Harry Potter was trying to score some crack.

"Ilya?" we asked, and he shot back into the shadows as if we had fired a gun. He nodded and led us to a nearby café, where I peppered him with questions about the military presence in the square. How were we going to pull off our flag stunt in the middle of level four of *Call of Duty: Modern Warfare 2*?

Ilya laughed and told me that we had nothing to worry about. We had arrived on November 8, the day after the ninetieth anniversary of the Bolshevik Revolution. Every year on that day, there is a grandiose military parade to mark the revolution. Because of this special anniversary, the troops had marched eleven thousand strong that year.

"Today not good day to sneak around," he told us in his thick Russian accent. "Tomorrow better." Ilya was very curious about our show. "You mock leaders on television? Without repercussion?" he asked. I explained that not only were there no repercussions, but sometimes the politicians even asked to come on the show to be made fun of. "Amazing!" he said.

"Now you have come to fly flag of your country in face of Putin's Kremlin, yes?" he asked, reading way too much into it.

"Something like that," I told him. Ilya said it would be impossible to do what we were planning without being stopped by the *politsiya*. "They watch everything in square. Once you fly flag, they will be on you. There is nothing I can do to help then, my friends. You will be doomed."

He was so much fun to hang out with. I tried to explain that it was just a little joke. If the cops came, then I would say that we were just taking a snap for some friends back home. No big deal.

"When you fly flag of freedom in front of the Spasskaya Tower? The Kremlin? Big deal." He spoke solemnly, as if he was bidding farewell to an old friend as he closed the lid on his coffin. Ilya seemed to think we were making some huge political protest, and if that was what it took to get him on board, it was fine with me.

I couldn't believe what I was seeing as we walked through Red Square. The Iron Curtain of my youth was lifted and now the window was flung wide open. St. Basil's Cathedral, the huge Main Department Store known as the GUM, the Kremlin and Lenin's Tomb were all laid out in front of me, real enough to touch. The soldiers that filled the square seemed to be as much in awe as I was. For most of them, the parade would be the only time in their life that they got to see Moscow.

Ilya asked a lot of questions about Canada and my job. What was it like to criticize your prime minister on television? Did I ever fear for my life? Had I met Anne Murray? My answers were far too boring for him and he mistakenly took my tediousness for modesty. I tried to change the topic by complimenting his English. I told him that he was missing some words and shared with him the unique slang of my home province of Newfoundland and Labrador. I taught him phrases like "How's she goin', b'y?" and "What are ya at, me son?"

He wrote each word down in his journal, slowly repeating them in his Russian accent: "What—are—you—at, boy?"

"Not 'boy,'" I told him. "'B'y.'" We didn't have time for *o*'s where I came from. He was fascinated with this gap in his linguistic knowledge and constantly asked me for more words to add to his lexicon. I imagined the shock of the next CNN journalist who met their Russian fixer for the first time, only to hear, "What are ya at, b'ys. Welcome to Russia. It's right wicked, me son."

The next day we met Ilya for a coffee at GUM. I felt as though he was giving me the last rites as we went through the plan for the day. Ilya would stay away from us as much as possible. The smaller our group, he reasoned, the better our chances at success. The last of the visiting soldiers were scattered around the square. We went for it.

First we made a few passes through the square to record a monologue. Adamm cuddled the camera close to him in his jacket as I tried my best to make it seem like I was either posing for a picture or chatting to my friend. We chose a spot and I dropped my backpack. I pulled out the tripod and flagpole and raised the big Canadian flag.

"Okay, Russia," I said to the camera. "You dropped a flag at the North Pole and you've claimed it as yours. So I dropped a Canadian flag in Red Square. We own Russia now. Your rules." Within a minute, the flashing lights of two *politsiya* cars came zooming towards us across the square. "Ilya!" I called out, like a lost child looking for its mother. I was going to need my translator.

The officer pulled my flag down and started yelling at us in Russian. The other officer took Adamm's camera and began to inspect it. Ilya approached cautiously and I pointed at him, saying, "Friend! Comrade! Comrade! Friend!"

"What are ya at?" Ilya said. "Will I tell them that today you fly flag in Putin's face, now?" he asked.

"No," I told my timid Tolstoy. "Just tell him that we travelled here from Canada because we love everything about Russia. Our friend was supposed to come with us but he couldn't because he was getting married. So we are just taking a picture with a Canadian flag to show him that we are thinking of him back home in Canada. Tell him we chose Russia over the wedding because Russia is so amazing."

Ilya translated as the Russian cops stared us down with a mixture of contempt and pity. "They have fallen for our ruse, me b'ys," he told us. "I also told them that I thought you were an idiot, so he would think me his comrade," he said, revelling in the unnecessary embellishment.

"He will not charge you, but we all must leave Red Square at once and never come back. Come on, we gets the frig out of this hole, me b'ys." And with that, our mission was complete. Almost.

We then took to the streets, "welcoming" Russians to their new Canadian home. I gave out doughnuts and Tim Hortons coffee. I gave away hockey jerseys. I traded with an elderly souvenir vendor we found selling his matryoshka dolls on Old Arbat Street. He gave me a doll and I gave him a shirt that said "Hey, Russia. Keep your hands off my pole." Ilya was delighted.

"There is a place where I must take you," he told me, slapping my back. We travelled across town to a small café in the basement of an austere building. The old wooden tables were filled with young men and women, deep in study as they scoured stacks and stacks of well-thumbed volumes of books. "These," my guide told me, his eyes afire, "are anarchists. This is a café for intellectuals." *Great*, I thought. *Russian nerds*.

"My friends," Ilya said, addressing the room, "this is the man I told you about, from Canada. He, too, is an intellectual. He thumbs his nose in Putin's face. Mark is like Canadian John Lennon. 'Imagine all the people,'" he quoted, "'living life in peace.' Mark, these are the b'ys."

They told me of the tensions that were beginning to boil over between Russia and Georgia and how they feared for their Georgian friends. Ilya told me that he had been inspired by what we had done. He, too, would protest, "Like Russian John Lennon."

I kept in touch with Ilya after I got home and was surprised when he wrote to tell me he had been arrested. He sent me a photo from a Russian newspaper. A cop stood in the foreground in riot gear, while Ilya and his friends were detained on a bus. Ilya's face was pressed to the window and his glasses were bent.

"Marvel! A picture of me—detained at the street protest yesterday," he wrote, adding a smiley face. "I am okay. I began to chant with all my might: 'We need another Russia.' I don't know if I screamed first. I clearly felt that it was my very loud cry that broke the avalanche. It was a wonderful feeling, very strong. The crowd chanted, riot police rushed to screw everyone. I heard nothing except my voice and the voice of the others who also chanted. I was grabbed from behind and dragged away by a man in civilian clothes. I stopped chanting. He turned me over to riot police, and I ended up on the bus with other people."

I had accidentally turned my translator into a revolutionary.

"The Basmanny Court was supposed to consider the case of how I called for the overthrow of the state system," he continued. "The court hearing is postponed but I am not going anyway; the charges: chanting appeals for revolution! But this is nothing compared to what we did, my friend, eh?" As a postscript he added, "What are you at these days, b'y?"

My trip to Russia reminded me of the incredible gift I had in being Canadian. I had a platform. I had access to the people who ran my country. I had the privilege of being able to criticize them to their face on television and they were expected to take it. But what was I really doing with that gift?

I felt as though I was a fraud. Ilya thought he had seen something in me that was not really there, but somehow, that mirage gave him the inspiration he needed to take a stand. It was I who admired him now. Ilya had become the person that he once hoped I was.

My career in comedy was beginning to take me all over the world. I had once been nervous about making a three-hour drive to Trinity. Performing in Halifax had once seemed like an insurmountable challenge. Travelling through the States made the places my father had dreamt of tactile and real. And Afghanistan had shown me a little of the true price of freedom. The farther I travelled, the more grateful I became to live where I did.

~

I would be reminded of my good fortune a year later when I travelled to Beijing for the 2008 Olympics. I was hired by CBC Sports to write and produce some segments for the Olympic broadcast. These pieces were intended to showcase some of the lighter sides of the Olympic experience. Once again, Pete Sutherland would join us as cameraman. Our fixer in Beijing was a young Chinese American man named Kyle. Kyle had travelled all over the world and he was an incredible guide.

We found ourselves shooting in Tiananmen Square, the site of the 1989 protests that had the whole world watching. However, I was shocked to discover that most of the people I chatted with in Beijing either didn't know the protests had happened or believed the whole thing to be some kind of Western hoax. As we filmed, I noticed that three "tourists" were following us. These men were Chinese nationals, dressed in brand-spanking-new bomber jackets and chinos. They were constantly taking pictures, but surprisingly, none were of the Gate of Heavenly Peace or the Monument to the People's Heroes. They were all of our crew. Kyle told us that we had better get used to them. They would probably be with us for the duration.

A couple of days later, we were shooting in a park. We were asking people to tell us about Chinese humour. We chatted with one elderly man who told us that the region of China that people made fun of was Dongbei. It was a funny chat because, as Kyle interpreted things for us, we began to realize that he was basically telling us the Chinese version of "Newfie jokes."

When Newfoundland joined Canada, a nation of impoverished fishers headed to the big cities like Toronto for work. They were greeted like newcomers often are, with derision and suspicion. This started a run on "Newfie jokes." These days, Canadians think of Newfoundland and Labrador as a province that supplies comedians, but back then, people thought of Newfoundlanders as the butt of every joke, not the deliverers of them. I remember seeing "Newfie joke" books for sale on the shelf at mainland drug stores when I first ventured there. These were not books of jokes by Newfoundland comedians. These were jokes about Newfoundlanders.

Q: How many Newfies does it take to screw in a lightbulb?
A: None. It will screw up their unemployment.

Q: Where do Newfies keep their trees?
A: Between their 2's and 4's.

Canadians told Newfie jokes. Slovenians told Ukrainian jokes. Americans used to tell Polish jokes. They are all the same jokes, just with another group substituted to make people feel superior in another part of the world. And now this man was telling us that these same jokes were being used to mock people from Dongbei, or, more evocatively, Manchuria.

A few minutes into this chat, all three of our "tourist friends" appeared out of nowhere. They had never approached us before. I stood in total shock as they began to speak to us in perfect English.

"This man is our uncle," one of them told us, placing his arm around the old man who had been telling us the jokes. The old man struggled to get away. It was clear that he did not know them. He was as much their uncle as I was. "He is wrong. He is very confused and must go now." Suddenly a white van pulled up. The "tourists" put the old man in the back of it as he pleaded with them and continued to struggle. The door shut and the van sped away. Our minders apparently did not like the idea of a Chinese national telling a Canadian audience that any of the Chinese people were lazy drunks. None of us felt much like laughing after that.

To help clear our heads, Kyle took us to Jiankou to see a crumbling section of the Great Wall built on a steep mountain ridge. This was nothing like the restored section you see in the travel brochures. Local farmers had taken much of the wall's building materials to use for their own walls and homes over the centuries and what was left made for a dangerous climb.

As we climbed, the skies opened and the rain poured down. Lightning struck the trees in the valley below and we found ourselves running for our lives. The locals call this section the "sky stairs" because they practically go straight up and they are so shallow it is almost impossible to obtain a foothold. I ran, slipping on the wet stones along the uneven pathways where a fall over the jagged edges and down the steep cliffs into the forest below meant certain death. Was it even possible to feel more alive than that? Or farther from home?

When the Olympics ended, *22 Minutes* asked if I would stay in China for another week to film a piece for the show. My friend and producer Geoff D'Eon flew over to take the wheel.

Newfoundland and Labrador premier Danny Williams was in the news at the time. He had been fighting with Ottawa, trying to get a fair deal for his province. I found one of his business cards in my wallet and I thought it might be fun to get some cheap copies made (when in China . . .) and see how far we could get impersonating a premier in a foreign country.

We recorded an interview at a Chinese radio station where I, as Danny, proposed separating and joining the People's Republic of China, as long as they would be open to renaming it the People's Republic of China, Newfoundland and Labrador.

We visited a school that taught students English. "Premier Williams" met with the students and taught them some Newfoundland phrases, much like I had done with Ilya in Russia. I had them all repeat "Stephen Harper can't be trusted" in unison.

We were having so much fun that we decided to visit the famous Lao She Teahouse. Geoff rented a black limo and placed Canadian flags on the hood to make it look more official. Kyle and Pete went ahead of us as Canadian media. When Geoff and I arrived, my heart sank. The entire staff were lined up outside to greet us.

Pete and I locked eyes as I got out of the car and he said, "You went too far this time." I shook hands with the staff as Kyle made the introductions. Geoff, posing as the premier's aide, and I soon found ourselves in a private room for an elaborate tea ceremony, where we were presented with gifts. I was shown a life-size statue of the owner shaking hands with President George H. W. Bush. I asked if I would be getting a statue as well. They politely said that they would look into that. I insisted that I pose with the owner so the sculptor would have something to work from. Then we were taken upstairs to the theatre and given front-row seats to a ninety-minute extravaganza.

The show featured Peking opera, a lion dance, shadow puppetry, a kung fu demonstration, the traditional art of face changing, in which colourful masks are switched in the blink of an eye, Handeng drumming, magic and more. I was asked to sign their impressive guest book alongside other VIPs like President Bush and Queen Rania of Jordan. Staying true to character, I took up a whole page with my signature. "To the Lao She Teahouse," I wrote, "Stephen Harper can't be trusted. Love, Premier Danny Williams."

We practically ran out of the place. I had been expecting our "tourist" friends to appear at any moment and toss us in the back of their van. The first thing I did when I got back to my hotel room was to call Premier Williams.

"Premier, hate to bother you but I'm in China. I dressed up as you and I might have given an interview saying you wanted to separate from Canada. I think I may have gone a bit far. I gave out your business cards."

"Say no more, Mark," the voice came crackling from ten thousand kilometres away. "If anybody asks, I'll just say it was me. Thanks for letting me know."

I cannot imagine getting that response from a politician anywhere else in the world.

~

I had long been interested in a man the media had dubbed "the Iraqi Jon Stewart." Ahmed al-Basheer is a household name in Iraq. The *Albasheer Show* is a news satire program with skits and desk jokes, just like *22 Minutes*. The main difference is that my targets were Canadian politicians. Al-Basheer's were ISIL and the Iraqi regime.

If I upset a politician, I might get a nasty phone call or an angry tweet. Ahmed was kidnapped for forty days. After receiving several more death threats, he moved his production to Jordan, a country that had about seven hundred thousand other Iraqi refugees at the time. From his new home, he lobbed jokes back into his homeland as if they were bombs. Each was a wound on the Iraqi regime and the terrorists he loved to hate. He amassed over twenty million views on YouTube.

"Laughter is the best way to unify people the world over," he has said. "It's smiling that makes us all human."

Ahmed told me that he would be killed if he tried to do what I did. His predecessor was an Iraqi comedian named Mahir Hassan. He sent up Saddam Hussein in a comedic film in the 1990s. When it aired on Kurdish television, Saddam ordered assassins to kill the entire cast. That's one hell of a tough review.

Ahmed invited me on his show, and I was amazed to see that it truly was an independent production. New death threats come in after every episode. Hearing that made nasty comments from right-wing trolls on my YouTube videos a little easier to take.

We wanted to get some scenic shots to start off the interview so we travelled to Petra, the "Rose City" of hand-hewn caves, temples and tombs that was lost for a millennium. We wanted to shoot in front of the iconic Treasury, which dates back to the first century AD. It is forty metres high and the rock facade is intricately carved.

Cory Gibson, my field producer for the trip, hired a fixer by the name of Abu Amir. We told Abu what we wanted to shoot, and he confidently told us not to worry. "My friends," he told us, "with Abu Amir, there is NO problem!"

I turned to Cory and said, "Whenever anyone talks like that, there always ends up being a problem."

We drove several hours with a number of stops at roadside shops and restaurants. Abu always needed to make a "quick visit," and I soon realized that he had a side hustle in which he took people who hired him to shops owned by people who had hired him to bring them the people who had initially hired him. We were shown knick-knack after knick-knack and drank cup after cup of tea. Whenever Cory reminded him that we were running out of time, Abu would smile his wide and bright smile and remind us that "with Abu Amir there is NO problem!"

We finally arrived in the town of Wadi Musa, which is two kilometres from the Petra site. This is where Abu Amir ran into a problem.

Officials were not happy that we had come to film without the necessary permits. They took us to the office of a local government official.
I asked if we were in some kind of trouble. "Don't worry," Abu Amir
told me. "With Abu Amir, there is NO problem!"

A serious-looking man sat behind an ornate desk, sweating in a
dark suit. Abu Amir looked very worried for someone with no problems. This made Cory and me worried, and soon the three of us were
looking very guilty indeed.

"He wants to know if we would like tea," Abu said.

I had been stopping to drink tea every twenty minutes for the last
four hours. "No, thanks. We really should get moving," I said.

Abu Amir looked as if I had just signed his death warrant. "You don't
understand," he told me through gritted teeth. "We MUST have the tea."

The official stared at me with a puzzled look on his face. How could
someone not want tea? I changed my position and nodded.

We drank in silence. Our host looked like a man who was expecting
to be either fired or killed or maybe both. Eventually, when the last
leaf of tea in the Hashemite Kingdom of Jordan had been consumed,
he spoke. He began to grill Abu Amir with the demeanour of an old
man who had seen his living room window broken by a neighbourhood kid's baseball one too many times.

Abu wriggled in his chair as I took in the room around me. On a
bookshelf there was a photo of the official with the Jordanian king.
Another showed him receiving some sort of plaque. And a third picture showed him meeting Prime Minister Stephen Harper. What were
the chances?

I turned on my phone and found a picture of myself with Harper.
I passed it to Abu Amir. "Here," I said, pointing at the framed photo
on the bookshelf. "Tell him I know that guy."

Abu Amir's mood changed significantly. "Is he a friend of yours?"
he asked, studying the photo.

"Something like that," I said. Harper had visited Jordan, pledging
$105 million in development aid. And he had recently appointed the

Mountie in charge of his personal security detail to the post of Canada's ambassador to Jordan. You know it's a tough country when you appoint a bodyguard ambassador.

The official studied the photo of me handing the prime minister a roll of toilet paper. I assume he thought that we must have been very close friends to fondle bathroom tissue so intimately together, because we were immediately given permission to film.

"This is very good," Abu told me. "He is giving us horses to finish the journey. See? With Abu Amir, there is NO problem!" There was one last thing, though. "Because your program is so well regarded, he would like to be interviewed for one half of an hour."

Cory set up the camera and Abu translated as we interviewed this sad, sweaty man for half an hour about the close ties between Jordan and Canada.

As soon as he finished, we were whisked away in horse taxis, the drivers wasting no time. We were pulled along between the towering two-hundred-metre-high walls of the narrow Siq canyon that hides the entrance to the long-forgotten wonder. A kilometre long and, at points, no more than three metres wide, the shaft opens at the end to reveal the ancient Nabataean city and that sight alone had made the journey worth it.

"My friends," Abu Amir shouted as we took in the wondrous sight, "I have a camel for you! No problem!" I shot my opening high atop a camel in front of the Treasury of Petra. There was no problem, after all. Abu Amir was a man of his word.

~

In Canada, a guy like me can walk up to the prime minister unannounced. The crowd will part. Legitimate journalists will even step aside and let me pass. The Mounties entrusted with the PM's safety will create a path for me, and the prime minister will stand there and take it as I make fun of him or her to their face. In Canada, this is not only tolerated but expected.

To many in oppressed societies, satire is a crime worthy of arrest or even death. When I think of Ilya, Ahmad al-Basheer and that old man in Beijing who disappeared in a white van, I am thankful for the gift of seeing what I get to do through the eyes of people for whom that reality does not exist.

11

AMERICAN REFUGEES

N 2010, IT FELT as though *22 Minutes* might be cancelled. The network had cut our order from eighteen to thirteen episodes per season. Newer shows, developed by fresh-faced executives, were always hungry for a prime-time slot, and few slots were better than ours. To be fair, the ratings had been sliding. Much of what we were doing was repetitive and stale. Luckily, we were able to persuade a former *22 Minutes* writer to come in and take over as showrunner.

Tim McAuliffe had left us to find his fortune in the States. He was doing pretty well at that, too. He had landed a job writing for *Late Night with Jimmy Fallon* and would go on to write and produce *The Office* for NBC. Tim pushed for the best material and the best ideas. That year, with Tim on board, we ended our shortened season with a Christmas special that garnered over one million viewers. The show was renewed with a full season, ensuring our twenty-two minutes of fame were not yet up.

The threat of cancellation made me uneasy, though. I was thirty-six, I had a family to provide for and I had been putting all my eggs in one basket. I was away from home for part of the year, every year, and I had missed so much. Cracks were beginning to appear in my home life, and it was becoming evident that Sherrie and I were growing apart. I began to wonder if it was time to make a change, and I started to think of a project all of my own. If I had imagined what that project would end up being, however, I would have raced back to the safety of *22 Minutes* and locked the door behind me.

In my career, I have had some very surreal experiences, but none has come close to matching the bizarre period I spent coupled with Randy and Evi Quaid. The Quaids were on the run from the law and at times they ran *to* me, *with* me and *from* me.

You probably remember Randy Quaid as the lovable and flaky Cousin Eddie in Chevy Chase's *Vacation* comedies, but there is much more to him than that. He should be remembered for his Oscar-nominated performance opposite Jack Nicholson in 1973's *The Last Detail*. He won a Golden Globe playing President Lyndon Johnson in *LBJ: The Early Years* in 1987. He appeared in popcorn-selling block-busters like 1990's *Days of Thunder* and 1996's *Independence Day*. In 2005 he starred in the groundbreaking film *Brokeback Mountain*. He was even a cast member for a season of *Saturday Night Live*. Randy Quaid was that rare performer who could do it all. He could make you laugh and he could make you cry.

When I met Randy in 2010, the state of his life would make you want to cry for him. His wife, Evi Motolanez, was a former model who twice appeared in *Vogue*. However, she wasn't doing much modelling when they met in 1998. Evi had been assigned as Randy's driver on a film. She got lost driving him to work on her first day. He proposed to her that same night, and the two went on to live a high-end Hollywood lifestyle, financed by Randy's endless train of film roles.

That train stopped in 2009. The Quaids were arrested for burglary and defrauding an innkeeper when they failed to pay a $10,000 bill at a hotel in Santa Barbara. Instead of paying it, they went on the lam. They were arrested a second time in 2010, this time for residential bur-glary when they were caught living illegally in a house they used to own in Montecito. Just like that, Randy and Evi went from Bogie and Bacall to Bonnie and Clyde and fled to Canada.

But the Quaids didn't just claim to be on the run from the law over unpaid hotel bills. They swore that they were running for their lives. They believed that assassins had killed two famous actor friends of theirs: *Kill Bill* star David Carradine and *The Dark Knight* star Heath Ledger. Carradine was found hanging in his closet. Ledger died of an accidental overdose. The Quaids claimed it was all a cover-up and said the two stars had been murdered by a league of assassins. This cabal of killers had a name. Randy and Evi were on the run from the Hollywood Star Whackers.

When I got wind of the situation, I knew that I could help them. After all, as every Canadian TV actor knows, the best place to hide from Hollywood is on Canadian television. *22 Minutes* contacted the Quaids through their Canadian lawyer. They had been living in their car in Vancouver, where the Canada Border Services Agency had started inadmissibility proceedings against them. The Quaids were now claiming refugee status, saying that if they returned to the States, the hit men would do to them what they had done to Carradine and Ledger.

Randy may have escaped the law, but now a dog was chasing him. Reality TV star Dog the Bounty Hunter was on the case. Duane "Dog" Chapman posted a video saying, "Randy Quaid. I'm coming for ya, bro." Chapman was famous for turning fugitives in to the police on TV. In Randy, he saw the ultimate prey who would earn him not only a big bounty but the even more lucrative prize of huge ratings.

Dog tweeted: "Attention Canada brothers & sisters please get me Randy Quad's [*sic*] address," adding, "Fe Fi Fo Fum look out Quaid here we come." What luck did I have getting to Randy, I wondered, if the most famous bounty hunter in the world couldn't find him? Then I saw a quote from Chapman where he said that he called himself Dog because "Dog is God spelt backwards."

Oh good, I thought, *Dog the Bounty Hunter is an idiot*. There was still hope.

We asked for an interview and, surprisingly, the Quaids agreed. They had been watching some of my work as they explored Canadian television. People who live in their cars are a great CBC demographic. People who find themselves in a hospital waiting room are also loyal viewers.

The Quaids had only one small demand: that the interview be conducted at the nineteen-thousand-seat Rogers Arena in Vancouver on the exact spot where Sidney Crosby had scored the gold Olympic goal in overtime against the Americans.

The *22 Minutes* field producer of the piece, Mark Mullane, was able to secure us fifteen minutes on the ice for part of the interview and talked the Quaids down from 10K in a baggie to a much smaller amount of cash and a new outfit for Randy.

Oh, there was one more demand. While Randy and I chatted, Evi wanted to circle us on the ice on skates, wearing a white bikini and flapping a big Canadian flag. Now, how could I say no to that?

I flew to Vancouver, not knowing what to expect. Did they really believe that these Star Whackers were out to kill them? Were they mentally stable? Would I fly across the country only to have nobody show up?

Mullane called me as soon as I landed. We had agreed to buy Randy a new outfit for the filming but he had picked out half of the store and the store was Holt Renfrew. Once again, Mark talked Randy down, this time to a couple of shirts. This gave me hope. They could be reasoned with. They were probably perfectly normal, I told myself. Maybe they were just misunderstood.

The Quaids then said that they would only meet us in a parking garage. I started to wonder if we were the ones who were going to end up whacked. We waited. And then we waited some more. We risked losing our scheduled time on the ice. If the Quaids wanted to become Canadian, they needed to learn that you don't mess with somebody's ice time.

Then, out of the darkness of the parking garage, they emerged, like Deep Throat in *All the President's Men*. They were bigger than life, like two cartoon characters. They reminded me of the Russian spies Boris and Natasha from the animated *Rocky and Bullwinkle* show. But while Boris and Natasha wanted to capture the moose, Evi and Randy wanted to become the moose. Evi carried Dojo, their Australian cattle dog, like a baby. It wiggled and twisted in her arms, just like you'd expect a dog that had been living in a car for the past month to. But when I compared their eyes, Evi seemed to be the wilder of the two.

We headed for the arena as I told them my plan. Everyone thought they were crazy. I didn't want to take advantage of them. I wanted to do my best to help them make their pitch to become Canadians.

I dressed Randy in a red-and-black-checkered lumberjack shirt with a blue trapper hat that made him look like his Cousin Eddie character in *National Lampoon's Christmas Vacation*. I wore a similar shirt and a hat with antlers. We were practically dripping maple syrup. Evi skated around us in her white bikini, the Maple Leaf proudly flapping from a flagpole in her arms. As promised, we stood on the ice where Sid the Kid had won us a victory over the United States. Would that golden magic happen a second time?

I asked him how long he had been in Canada. He said he had been here for about a month. That reminded me of the Liberal leader at the time, Michael Ignatieff. The Conservatives were running an ad reminding Canadians that Ignatieff had been living away for thirty-four years. The ad claimed the Liberal leader was "just visiting."

"Leaving America and living here for a month," I said, "you are now qualified to become the Liberal leader of Canada." He clearly had no idea what I was talking about, but he played along. I asked him if he had ever thought about entering politics. I wanted to know what he would do if he was ever elected prime minister.

"As your prime minister," he nervously began, "I will make sure that everyone gets heat."

"You know," I said, "that is probably the best speech a Canadian prime minister has ever given us."

He told me that he had spent his first week in Canada in jail, and I was curious to know what Canadian jail was like.

"I had a place to lie down," he told me. "Like a dressing room. I felt like I was on a movie."

"When Randy Quaid is in the jail, he thinks of it as a dressing room," I laughed. "So going to court is just like doing a guest spot on *Law & Order*."

Things were going great. Randy was coming off as personable and, well, sane. Then Evi skated over. She thought we were having too much fun. She wanted to talk about the life-and-death predicament she believed them to be in.

"What's happened is for three years, slowly, ex-accountants, lawyers and business managers, who were working together to steal Randy's money, and we're talking about forty million, were genuinely trying to kill us."

This wasn't endearing or funny. I quickly proceeded to ask Randy some questions from the Canadian citizenship test. I had given him the answers beforehand. I wanted to shock the viewers and give Randy a chance to look good for the camera.

"What is the name of the prime minister of Canada?" I asked.

"Steve Harper," he proudly answered.

"What did the Hudson's Bay Company control?" I asked.

Randy paused for effect. "They controlled the fur trade," he answered, a twinkle in his eye.

I asked him the year of Confederation.

"Oh, come on," he laughed. "1867."

I then gave him one last important test. I threw a punch, and Randy, having taken many a big-screen smack in his life, sold it perfectly. He stood, looking confused as he rubbed his jaw.

"Before you get mad," I said, "I want you to think like a Canadian. I just hit you. What should you say?"

Randy thought for a moment. Then he stared right down the lens. "I'm sorry?"

I shook his hand. "Welcome to Canada, buddy," I said. Our piece was finished. There was nothing wrong with this guy.

We left them in their parking garage but I couldn't help worrying about them on the long flight back home. Something troubled me. Whenever Evi had started to talk Star Whackers, I could sense Randy bristle slightly. He would sometimes say, "Aw, come on, Evi," and "Why do we have to say that?" It was as if a fog had lifted and a different man had woken up and now wondered where he was and how he had gotten there. At that point, Evi would pull him away, out of earshot and out of sight. When they returned, Randy would be much quieter and the twinkle in his eye would have faded. He no longer argued.

The piece aired to huge success both for us and for them. Randy and Evi were very happy with the way things had gone. They continued to contact me, though it wasn't always easy to communicate. They were constantly changing emails and phone numbers.

But the Quaids weren't the only famous people who had seen the piece. Dog the Bounty Hunter started following me—but luckily, only on Twitter. Each week, millions would tune in to watch him chase down crooks in Hawaii. Dog was impressed that I had found a way to reach the Quaids and wanted to talk to me. He asked for my number. Dog the Bounty Hunter had slid into my DMs.

One night I was jolted awake when my cellphone rang. There are a lot of time zones between Hawaii, where he lived, and Halifax. I reached for my phone in the dark, knocking over a glass of water in the process. I answered, half-asleep and angry. "Who is it?"

"Brah," said a somewhat familiar voice on the other end of the line. "It's Dog, brah!" I sat up in the dark like a shot, suddenly very much awake. "Is this Mark?"

"It is, brah," I heard myself say, not quite sure what it was that I was saying. "I mean, yes. You have reached Mark Critch. How may I help you?"

"You've got to help me get to Randy, brah," he said. "He needs to come to justice. Randy trusts you, brah. Now you gotta trust me, okay, brah?" I wasn't following the logic here. Randy trusted me so I had to trust Dog? So that he could arrest the guy that trusted me?

"Look," I told him, "I don't really want to get involved. I'm sure you can find him on your own if I could."

"I can't get a bad guy in Canada, brah," he explained. This was true. Dog had arrested Andrew Luster, a Max Factor heir, in Mexico. Luster had jumped a $1-million bond on charges that he drugged and raped three women. But bounty hunting was illegal in Mexico, and Dog was charged with "deprivation of liberty" (also known as kidnapping) in Puerto Vallarta. He was also not legally able to bounty-hunt in Canada.

"Only you can help me, brah," Dog pleaded. "Get them into a car. Bring them to the border and I can pull them over."

No frigging way, brah. I wasn't about to trick someone into being pulled over a border. Not even people I had only just met. Yes, the Quaids were on the run, but they were harmless. And I didn't want to be seen in an episode of *Dog the Bounty Hunter*, flashlights shining into the lens, Tasers crackling, as Dog yells, "Where did he go, brah? There he is! He's hiding under the baby pool!"

Dog had said something that resonated with me. He'd said, "Randy trusts you." And he did. He took a chance with our interview. He was in Canada now and I was content to let Canadian justice deal with him, not a bounty hunter who couldn't carry a real gun because he was a convicted felon.

"Okay, brah," Dog said dejectedly. "If you want to rock 'n' roll, we got the guitar. This is good versus evil." Maybe it was, Dog. And maybe you didn't realize what side you were really on.

I contacted the Quaids the next day and told them about my chat with the bastard child of Don Ho and Boba Fett. The stakes could not be higher for them: Canadian residency or American prison. They believed that they were truly refugees and everything hung on a successful immigration hearing. I began to concoct a plan.

What if we shot a series where we took them across the country? We would travel from coast to coast to coast, along the way taking a crash course on what it means to be Canadian. And each week, Canadians could watch and decide for themselves if these were the kind of people we need in Canada.

We'd go from the kitchen parties of Newfoundland to the dog-sled races of Manitoba. We'd travel from the log cabins of BC to take French classes in Quebec. The Quaids would take odd jobs in each locale and maybe even find a place to call home. We would move from the east coast to the west coast, all the while inching closer to the dramatic conclusion of their immigration trial.

I pitched the idea to the Quaids and they were in. Tim McAuliffe joined me as a writer, and we set to work coming up with pitches. We put a package together and we took it to the CBC. They green-lit a pilot and we were off to the races. This was not *The Amazing Race*, however. It was more of an eh-mazing race.

The most exciting part for me would be to visit the town of Haskell, Quebec. The town is right on the border between the United States and Canada. And when I say it's on the border I mean literally. The border runs straight through the middle of the town and even runs through some buildings. One of those buildings is the town library. That is where I wanted the Quaids to meet Dog the Bounty Hunter. We would sit on our respective sides of the border, a foot away from each other, where Dog could make his case. That was great TV.

We went about planning the first episode. Newfoundland and Labrador's lieutenant-governor, former federal minister John Crosbie, agreed to meet the Quaids at Government House. We would introduce the Quaids to my friend Gordon Pinsent, who knew a thing or two about immigration himself. Gordon was born in the Dominion of Newfoundland, before we joined Canada in 1949. He immigrated to Canada to find work as an actor.

I was also going to take the Quaids to the Association of New Canadians where they would meet other people who were applying to become Canadian. How did the Quaids' story compare with more traditional refugee stories?

I'd take them on a crab boat so they could experience the hard work that brought so many people to that rocky island. Later that night, I'd take them to a bar where my friend Alan Doyle, then with his group Great Big Sea, would lead a traditional music session. Randy would perform a song he'd written with the band. Of course, the song would be called "Star Whackers."

Locations were found, Visas were applied for and a crew was assembled. Now all I needed was the Quaids. But Evi refused to get on the plane from Vancouver. She was worried that it would be diverted to the States, where they would be arrested. Or what if the Americans sent jets to force the plane into American airspace? No, she felt a plane was too dangerous. She wanted them to drive to Newfoundland from Vancouver in their Prius.

Things were not going to plan, but they were kind of going as expected. They started to spin out of control. I flew out to Vancouver with the show's producer to try to calm them down. Once again, we met cloak-and-dagger style, waiting for their car/home to pull up from an alley. They wanted to eat in a fancy restaurant. But they wanted their dog to come too. And they wanted us to buy their dog a steak dinner or they wouldn't agree to the meeting. One very well-fed dog later, and we were all sitting around a table hashing things out while looking over our shoulders for phantom killers.

We talked for hours, but nothing of substance was said. They trusted me, but not the executives and lawyers. The longer we talked, the more it became clear that this show was never going to happen. Once, when Evi got up from the table to let the dog relieve itself, Randy turned to me apologetically. "Look," he said as he stared down at the napkin on his lap, "I know this is all crazy. I don't mean to be trouble. It's just . . . Evi, you know? She gets these ideas and I don't know what's real or not but she loves me, you know? And I love her so much. So I go along with it. I know it's all crazy, but I can't leave her. I can't. You know?"

I did know. This show was never going to happen. Not because they didn't want to do it, but because they just weren't able to.

Evi came back to the table. "Let's throw your idea out and start over," she said, babbling like a broken faucet. "No more of this reality stuff. We can write a script. You can play my father. He was Canadian FBI!"

"We don't have the FBI in Canada," I told her, desperate to kill her idea gently. "Do you mean CSIS?"

"Whatever it is you call it up here," she continued, frustrated with my interruption. "You can be my father and you're chasing me and Randy and we can play ourselves and—"

"Wait a minute," I said, as this new piece of information began to develop in my mind like a darkroom negative. "Was your father really born in Canada?"

"Yes!" she shouted, throwing her hands up in the air. "But that's not important! What's important is that he was Canadian FBI!"

I dropped my head into my hands. "Evi," I began, "if your father was born in Canada, then why would you need refugee status? I'm no immigration lawyer but you can apply for citizenship because your father is Canadian. And Randy can apply because he's married to you."

Not long after, CBS News reported: "Randy and Evi Quaid Set Free in Canada, and She's Declared a Citizen!" "During Thursday's hearing," the story said, "Evi Quaid repeatedly said her father was a Canadian FBI agent—a claim she explained later by saying her father was a Canadian who moved to the U.S. and began working for the FBI . . .

"On the other hand, her actor-husband Randy, who hails from Texas, is also no longer in detention, but will have to proceed through further immigration channels."

So much for my show. Randy and Evi, however, were not going to give up as easily as I was. They wanted to come live with me and create their new show called *Star Whackers* in which I would play a Mountie.

They wrote a script in which Evi's character is a prostitute who makes love to my Mountie character while Randy watches on a video screen from his penthouse suite in Whistler. One day I got an email from Randy that said, "New Name for the show—THE QUAID CRITCH LOST WEEKEND VIEWING FOR NUMBNUTS." This was not something I wanted to sign up for. I was out.

The production company tried to keep going without me. They arranged to film Randy as he performed with a band in Vancouver. He finally debuted his "Star Whackers" song, and when the song was finished, he added a message of thanks, saying, "Thank you to the Canadian Council for Refugees and all the great work they do, for opening their facilities . . . for refugees to come into this country. And thank this great nation of Canada for leaving the light on."

It was lights out for Randy, however, as his request to become a Canadian citizen was denied.

In 2015, Randy and Evi were picked up while trying to drive across the Canadian border into Vermont, less than one week before his deportation date. The charges against them were dropped and they were freed without bail. Dog the Bounty Hunter was not there to welcome them home.

Maybe Randy is better off in the United States after all. He became an ardent Trump supporter. In the waning days of his presidency, Donald Trump retweeted a series of Randy's bizarre videos.

"Wake up, you sleeping giant," Randy ranted in one video. "The Lilliputians have tied you down with their fantastic dreams of icebergs melting into dinosaurs and train tracks stretching across the Pacific waters. Trump trumpets reveille!"

"Thank you Randy," the president of the United States tweeted, "working hard to clean up the stench of the 2020 Election Hoax."

Try as I might, I could not legitimize Randy Quaid. It seems he eventually met his saviour in Donald Trump. I guess it takes one to know one. Randy even threatened to run for Congress in California. "That swamp needs cleaning up big time," he tweeted, "I should know. I have serious winning experience emptying the sh***ers for that district," referring to his famous line from *National Lampoon's Christmas Vacation*.

I don't know if that will ever happen, but I do know that Randy loves Evi more than anything in the world. I wish them both happiness and I know that they will only ever be happy together. So, Randy and Evi, wherever you are, be you running for office or running from the law—long may you run.

12

BAYWATCHED

I SAT AT MY PARENTS' kitchen table, patiently listening to their every word. That was a telltale sign something was up.

"What's wrong with you?" my father asked midsentence from behind the newspaper he read while he listened to the radio.

"Why would anything be wrong?" I asked, putting off the inevitable for a few seconds more.

"You're listening to me."

The jig was up.

In 2013, Sherrie and I decided to break up. It was a difficult decision but the right one for both of us. She's a great mother and we are all lucky to have her in the family.

One of the hardest things to figure out was how to tell people. Gwyneth Paltrow and Chris Martin "consciously uncoupled." Justin Theroux and Jennifer Aniston had a "gentle separation." Channing Tatum and Jenna Dewan "reached the end of a magical journey." Sherrie and I "broke up."

I was worried about telling my parents. They were old-school Catholics. I had already given them two grandchildren out of wedlock. Now the relationship itself was in flames, not unlike hellfire.

I had gone to their house to spill the beans. Beans had never been spilled before at our kitchen table. Tea had, and milk, surely. But never beans. We Critches were not known to open up. We liked things kept shut, and preferred our beans stored safely in the cupboard.

"Sherrie and I are splitting up," I mumbled and braced myself for the inevitable litany of reasons why we should stay together, from "think of the children" to "think of what the neighbours will say." Anything but "think what's best for you."

"Good god," my father said from behind his newsprint shield. "About time."

"What?" I said. Surely I had heard him wrong.

"Any fool knew that wasn't going to last. You're too different. Want a cup of tea?"

And with that, our heart-to-heart was over and the beans went back in the can.

The hardest moment of it all was sitting down with Sherrie to tell our sons that we would be splitting. I had been dreading the moment for months. We had done a good job of hiding our disagreements from them. Maybe we had done too good a job, because neither had seen it coming. Try as I might to explain, the words just wouldn't come. I felt as though I had failed miserably in the only job I ever had that really mattered.

"It's okay," Will said as he comforted his older brother. "We're still a family and we'll still all love each other. You don't have to live in the same house to be a family." He was just ten years old but he had a much better handle on things than I did at forty. We had done a pretty good job as parents, after all.

I found myself spending Christmas in a ground-floor apartment. The walls were thin enough to hear the phone ringing in the apartment above. I began to know my upstairs neighbours intimately. They liked *The Price Is Right*. They went to bed at eleven. They shuffled to the bathroom at bedtime. They ran to it at six a.m. I once heard a voice say, "The guy downstairs is a lot quieter than the last guy was." I wore my stealth as a badge of honour. In fairness, though, it's easy to be quiet when you don't want to do anything but lie on the couch and watch *Downton Abbey* on an iPad with earphones.

My best friend Tristy knew I was a plant that needed some watering.

Tristy is a videographer and was finishing up his scheduled shoots for the holidays. We made a plan to do some Christmas shopping downtown. That usually meant walking halfway up one side of Water Street as we half-interestedly eyed the window displays, then popping into the Duke of Duckworth pub for a pint, then ambling up the other side of the street, pausing every now and then to pensively admire a pair of mitts or a scarf in a shop window, and making our way up to the Republic pub for another pint. After a few zigzags up and down the street, we would self-diagnose as "too drunk for Christmas shopping" and retire to a pub for some festive drinking.

As I was gearing up for a much-needed dose of Christmas cheer, Tristy called. "Bad news, me buddy," he apologized over the line, "I've got to do a shoot."

"What's up?" I asked, hoping to get the scoop on some juicy political scandal.

"Pamela Anderson just called a press conference at the Canadian Sealers Association." That was the kind of thing I would have expected Tristy to say *after* we had been drinking.

Pamela Anderson, the former star of TV's *Baywatch*, had come to my island home to try to end the seal hunt. Before this visit, the only kind of Baywatch we had in Newfoundland was the kind where people watch the actual bay.

(We open on a rocky beach. Two older men in cable-knit sweaters look to the sea. They cannot actually see the sea, because of thick fog. A small boat makes its way across the bay.)

FISHERMAN 1: Who's that? Is that John Hearn's boat?

FISHERMAN 2: No. That's Steve Lee.

FISHERMAN 1: Thought he lost his licence.

FISHERMAN 2: He did.

FISHERMAN 1: Fair enough.

FISHERMAN 2: Yes, b'y.

End scene.

But now, for the first time in history, the baywatchers would become the baywatched. Anderson was indeed on the island, and she was accompanied by Sam Simon, the co-creator of *The Simpsons*. Simon was going to offer a $1-million incentive to buy out sealing licences. I couldn't believe it. Not only had I lost a perfectly good afternoon of Christmas-shopping procrastination, but these two were insulting the intelligence of everyone in the province.

A million dollars may sound like a lot of money, but with around six thousand sealers in the union, Simon and Anderson's offer would amount to only about $167 each. If people like Sam Simon and Pamela Anderson seriously wanted to buy off six thousand people, they easily could. And that's without PETA and Greenpeace or any of the other organizations sitting on millions of dollars in donations to "Save the Seals" chipping in. But they don't want to do that. Because without a seal hunt, the donations that they rely on would stop. This was nothing more than a publicity stunt meant to generate headlines right before the holidays. I was supposed to be licking my wounds and enjoying some time off over the holidays, but Pam's visit was like the Bat-Signal shining over Gotham City.

It always irked me that people like Pamela Anderson used images of baby seals to fundraise. The whitecoat baby seals have not been hunted since 1987. I say stop misleading people. Lose the term "baby" altogether. Rename the species. Marketing 101. Change the name from baby seal to ice rat. Nobody wants to kill a baby seal. Everybody wants to kill an ice rat. Nobody is donating to a "Save the Ice Rat" campaign, no matter what you picture on the flyer.

People have been eating seal meat and wearing seal fur since back when you didn't have the luxury to pick your food based on looks. They did it, as Inuit there have for thousands of years, because it was the only source of protein for much of the year. They did it because, if they didn't, they would die.

These days, though, the demand for seals has dropped substantially. The hunt for all of Canada culls around 66,800 seals. That's out of around eight million harp seals bobbing around in the Atlantic. With demand plummeting, the hunt is no longer a going concern. Sealers don't make much money at it. The only people making money off the seal hunt are the people trying to stop it.

We are used to celebrities showing up in Newfoundland and Labrador to help save their careers—I mean, the seals. First it was Brigitte Bardot in the 1970s. She was a French pin-up and actress, the Pamela Anderson of her day. Years later, she faced prosecution for inciting racial hatred when she referred to the native inhabitants of the French island of Réunion as "aboriginals who have kept the genes of savages" and a "degenerate population." Indigenous people? Not so much. But seals? She loved seals.

Even Paul McCartney came to Newfoundland and Labrador. He couldn't save the Beatles, but he tried to save the seals. In 2006, he and his then wife, Heather Mills, cuddled baby seals on the ice pans for the cameras. Well, what they obviously didn't know is that a mother seal will often reject a baby seal if it's covered in a human scent. So it's very possible the first baby seal killed in the 2006 seal hunt goes to Paul McCartney.

Sir Paul even went on *Larry King Live* to debate then Newfoundland and Labrador premier Danny Williams about the seal hunt. Williams invited McCartney to come to Newfoundland to meet sealers and learn about the impact a ban would have on working-class people. "I want you to come to Newfoundland and Labrador," the premier said. "I want you to know the truth and the facts. And I'm certain that you will partner with us and move this forward because I think we can convince you that this is a very humane undertaking."

At this McCartney bristled, saying, "Well, we're here, Danny. You don't need to invite us. Thanks for the invitation, but we're here. We're actually in the studio here. We are in Newfoundland. And we saw the seals yesterday."

"First of all, Paul," the premier calmly explained, "you're in Prince Edward Island now. And I'm in Newfoundland and Labrador." Beatle Paul had been in Newfoundland earlier in the day, but now, seemingly unawares, he was in a completely different province. That moment pretty much sums up celebrity understanding of the seal hunt.

Now it was Pamela Anderson and Sam Simon, and this time they brought a cheque! Well, if it was publicity they were after, I figured I would try and help them get some. I grabbed my chequebook and headed out into the freezing St. John's afternoon.

I stood on the sidewalk of the building that housed the Canadian Sealers Association and watched the pandemonium. Tristy and a large gaggle of other journalists struggled to find a clear shot of the tableau. Dan Mathews, the senior vice-president of People for the Ethical Treatment of Animals, shouted that it was time to end the killing of "baby seals." A few angry sealers heckled in protest, calling the PETA VP a liar.

Some of St. John's finest from the Royal Newfoundland Constabulary looked on from the sidelines, trying to figure out who, if anyone, needed protection from whom. In the centre of it all stood Pamela. She wore heels and I, in my slush-covered boots, wondered how she could still be standing.

Her head was wrapped in a white cloth and she wore large dark sunglasses, the kind you would expect a movie star to wear. The stark white fabric that covered her head was contrasted by her big dark shades, and the more I stared at her, the more I thought she looked like a baby seal herself.

Sam Simon stood next to her. He was gaunt and clearly not well. Simon had been diagnosed with terminal cancer and had decided to spend a portion of his sizeable fortune on animal-rights causes. The two out-of-place American millionaires held a giant novelty cheque, the kind usually reserved for children's hospital telethons and Publishers Clearing House sweepstakes. It was if they were saying, "Hey, ya dumb Newfies! It's your lucky day! Look! Real live celebrities with a million dollars! Bet you never saw that before!"

"You can spend the money any way you want to," Simon said, though nobody felt like playing along with this particular round of Simon Says. "You can get a nice dinner at the Keg. Or even go get drunk on beer on George Street."

And with that, my blood started to boil just as if it had been in a kettle. I was not having a great month to begin with, and now this guy was insulting Newfoundlanders and Labradorians with the offer of a free drink.

I had ambushed celebrities and many press scrums in the past, but always for comedic purposes, and always for the show with my own camera. Not this time. This time, I just wanted to make a point.

I walked past the sealers and the reporters and straight up to Simon and Anderson. I was waving a million-dollar cheque of my own. Mine was not Ed McMahon–sized. It was out of my own chequebook and it was real. Pamela Anderson had said that videos of the seal hunt made her "embarrassed to be Canadian." If Pamela Anderson had come to Newfoundland with a million-dollar cheque because she had been so upset by horrific videos of the seal hunt, then I was going to make her an offer out of her own playbook.

"We've all seen the cruel videos," I said. "*Barb Wire, Baywatch Nights, Barbarella.*"

"*Stripperella*," Anderson corrected me. In the heat of the moment, I had inadvertently referenced Jane Fonda's sci-fi film instead of Anderson's animated film about a crime-fighting stripper.

"*Stripperella*, sorry, thank you," I apologized. "They make *me* embarrassed to be a Canadian." I turned to Pamela. "I'll make you the same offer. I'll give you a million dollars to stop acting."

The PETA VP was getting nervous, trying to laugh me off while he motioned for the police officers to swoop in and remove this interloper who was stealing his publicity stunt with a better-thought-out publicity stunt. The cops didn't move.

"Is that cheque real?" Anderson asked me, and I assured her it was, before reminding her of her own math.

"I'll give you the same offer you made the sealers," I continued while the sealers cheered and the cameras clicked. "There are so many members of the sealers' association, it breaks down to $165 a person. Will you give up your livelihood for $165?"

I don't really know what she thought of that. Her eyes were hidden behind her dark seal-like sunglasses, and I'm pretty sure her ability to express surprise had left her several Botox sessions ago. But I knew

I had made my point, and I knew what the clip on the evening news would be now.

"Aren't you going to say anything to him?" the frustrated PETA VP shouted to two cops who were shivering close by.

"Yes, I am," one of the cops said as he walked towards me, removing a glove. "I'm going to say I'd like to shake your hand." He stretched out his hand, and I shook it just long enough so that our hands didn't freeze together, and then I gave Mr. PETA the standard Newfoundland nod and a wink. "Welcome to Newfoundland," I said, and walked off.

I wandered over to Tristy's truck and leaned against the hood as I watched Sam and Pam slide the giant cheque under the door of the sealers association. There was nobody there to take it. The office was closed on Tuesdays. But they already knew that. This was all just for show. Nobody really wanted the seal hunt to end. Their offer was the same as mine: a safe one to make because you knew the other person would never accept it. And even if they did, it'd be worth it because you just can't buy publicity like that.

While I waited for Tristy to file his story, I watched Sam Simon struggle to climb into his waiting car. We disagreed, and I thought him disingenuous, but I admired him for choosing to spend his final days fighting for something he believed in.

He passed away not long after, but six years later, Newfoundland and Labrador was haunted by him one last time. *The Simpsons* aired an episode in which Lisa visits Canada. The character Ralph Wiggum declares, "I'm a Newfie," before clubbing the head off a stuffed seal. Of course it was a baby seal.

13

THE CLOSET

THE FIRST FEW TIMES I met Stephen Harper, I tried to avoid him. Not because I didn't like him. Back in 2003, when he was the leader of the Canadian Alliance party, he was always trying to get some screen time. Even when he became leader of the Conservative Party, Harper would see us on the Hill chasing after some Liberal cabinet minister and say, "Hey! Do you guys need me for something?"

We usually didn't. Most road trip pieces for the show are about two minutes long. Three minutes would be a very large chunk of real estate. But when someone is staring at you with his perfectly combed hair and cold yet hopeful shark eyes, it's very hard to say no, so sometimes we would shoot a few minutes with Harper that we knew would never make it into the piece. Then, the next time we were up on the Hill, he would invariably come over and say, "Hey, you didn't use me in your show last week." And so we would shoot something that we wouldn't use in the next week's show, and so on and so on.

One weekend in Ottawa, just as we finished shooting a piece, we came across Stephen Harper in the empty halls of Parliament. "Hey," he shouted across the chasm, "you guys need me for anything?"

"Oh, crap," cameraman Pete muttered under his breath. I turned to see the bright-eyed and bushy-tailed party leader walking towards us with folders and folders of documents under his arms.

"I'm the only one up here working this afternoon," he said. "Maybe you guys could make a funny piece about that." I looked to Pete and he gave me the look. He seemed to be saying, "Don't do this. This always happens. We are done. Let's go get a beer. We will never use this."

"Sure," I said, feeling guilty. "What do you have in mind?"

"I'll show you how hard I'm working," he suggested. Hilarious. So we climbed the stairs to his office, where one other person was working with him. He introduced us. He joked a bit about how hard he works on behalf of Canadians. And after about twenty minutes, we left and I bought Pete several hoppy beers to make up for wasting his time.

I would kill to have that footage now. But, sadly, we never used it. When you meet a new MP or a newly minted party leader, you never stop to think that you might be speaking to a future prime minister.

In 2006, Stephen Harper became Canada's twenty-second prime minister, and I was there. I was able to nab him for a moment, congratulate him on his win and jokingly remind him that all the jokes we'd made about him in the past were just jokes. I asked him to leave us alone if he planned to cut the CBC.

He told me not to worry. I turned to the camera and said, "We're so screwed."

And so we were. We were pushed off the Hill, blocked from attending events, and we found ourselves unable to get anywhere near the man. Once, when fellow *22 Minutes* host Geri Hall tried to ask Harper a question at a press conference, she found herself handcuffed by the RCMP, despite her press pass. Times had changed.

You won't be surprised to hear that I was less than sad when Harper was defeated in 2015 after nearly a decade of governance. In fact, I decided to leave him a cheeky farewell. It had become known that visitors to the House of Commons sometimes stole the nameplate from Justin Trudeau's seat. It had become so common that he had taken to autographing the back of it, so the thief would have a surprise memento. Once, when I found myself on the floor of the House, I signed the back of Harper's. On one side it read "Harper, The Right Hon. Stephen Joseph," and on the other it read "Mark Critch."

On the day Harper stepped down, I was in Burlington, Newfoundland and Labrador, population 314. My friend Shaun Majumder grew up there and each summer he hosted a festival of food, music and comedy. Shaun and I would perform in a comedy night, and hundreds of tourists would camp out in the scenic little town.

Cellphone coverage in Burlington is not great. In fact, there's just one spot, down from the fire hall and up from the concert site, where you can get a signal. A rock had been brightly painted and the words "phone rock" were scrawled on it in white paint. The rock did not lie. When you stepped on it, you could get crystal-clear telephone reception and you could download whatever your Wi-Fi-less heart desired. But the second you stepped off it, you were transported back into the dark ages of rotary-dial telephones and beepers.

I stood on the phone rock and contemplated a tweet on the topic of Harper's resignation. I thought of perhaps posting a picture to Instagram of that nameplate with my signature on the reverse. That seemed petty to me, though.

So instead, I posted a picture of me standing in the broom closet where the prime minister had hidden for fifteen minutes during the 2014 shootings at Parliament Hill by Michael Zehaf-Bibeau. Harper later said he felt remorse for ducking into the closet to hide. He needn't have. He was apparently following the orders of those who were there to guard him.

I didn't expect the picture to be explosive. The closet had become a popular spot for people on the Hill to get their picture taken. The *Huffington Post*'s Ottawa bureau chief Althia Raj posted a picture of herself and Conservative Senator Mike Duffy in the closet. "Caption contest!" she tweeted along with the photo. NDP MP Ryan Cleary tweeted a photo of himself and three others in the closet, saying "it was the go-to place" during a Christmas party on the Hill. I captioned my photo: "Stephen Harper stepped down. Here I am in his closet." And then I posted it without hesitation. *Farewell to Stephen Harper and on to making fun of Justin Trudeau for a few years*, I thought. Then I went to bed.

I woke to a beautiful summer's day. I chatted with the locals and waved to the tourists as I made my way to the phone rock. In the distance, I could hear the band that would perform that night doing a sound check. Everything was right in the world. I stood on the phone rock and leaned this way and that, trying to catch some cell reception as if it was a butterfly and my phone was the net. My phone sprang to life, shaking vigorously like a hummingbird suffering a seizure. It was impossible to check any individual message before another dozen notifications opened up on the screen, like a classroom of children told that they were about to get ice cream, all screaming, "Me first!"

I finally picked one headline that seemed to sum the situation up nicely. The *Huffington Post* wrote: "Mark Critch Photo Mocking Harper Is a 'F**king Embarrassment.'"

What the hell had happened? I thought posting the cheeky picture on Instagram would be safe. Twitter is for political hacks, trolls and destroying yourself. Instagram is for pictures of your food and vacations.

The story began, "Conservative MP Michelle Rempel ripped into a CBC comedian for mocking Stephen Harper during 2014's Parliament Hill shooting." It went on to share her response to the photo I posted.

> "I don't really have words to describe my disgust at this post of yours," Rempel wrote in a series of tweets.
>
> "May you never have to experience hearing gunshots coming towards you while you're in a confined space. May you never have to choose between running for your life or trying to protect your friends from the unknown. May you never have a panic attack in a movie [that] has gunshots in it two years after running for your life . . . What you posted isn't satire, or comedy. It's a fucking embarrassment."

The *Globe and Mail* headline read, "MP Accuses Comedian of Triggering Her with Mocking Photo of Stephen Harper." The story repeated many of the same points as the other article, adding, "The photo and Rempel's reaction late Friday triggered a flood of debate on social media that continued through Sunday afternoon. Some people accused Critch of showing poor taste while others criticized Rempel for over reacting."

A great Twitter war had erupted with hundreds of tweets that either felt Michelle was out of line or called for my head.

I felt a tap on my shoulder. I turned to find a guy wearing one of those straw hats you get free with a case of Corona. "Hey, buddy," he said, "quit hogging the phone rock." A line of people had formed, all hoping to stand where I was standing, though I'm sure that not a single one would have wanted to be in my shoes.

"He's not even talking to anybody," he said to the woman behind him. "He's just checking his Twitter." I felt like I was back in the eighties, arguing over a phone booth. Realizing that I was running out of time, I opened my DMs to reach out to Michelle and apologize. I was surprised to find that she had already sent a message to me. She said that she was sorry for swearing and went on to tell me about her experience on the day of the shooting. Hearing her story put the whole thing into context for me. I immediately regretted the photo. I told her that I was sorry for being so cavalier and thoughtless. We chatted, privately, without an audience, the way people did before social media.

I told her that she needn't apologize to me. I loved an MP who swore and I deserved every word she had tweeted in my direction. To be honest, I hadn't thought how my post might affect someone who had been there that day. As we too often do, I didn't think much of anything about what I had posted. I deleted the picture, but the internet never forgets. Unless, that is, you do something good.

"Come on, buddy," the man behind me shouted, having become the human equivalent of a beeping car horn. "We all have places to go." I looked at him and doubted his claim very much. But I relented. I stepped down from the rock, but I was still hanging from my cross. I needed a drink, but Burlington was a religious town and this was a dry event. No cell service and no booze. I really knew how to pick a place to have a crisis.

Later, once the afternoon concert began and the crowd was busy, I returned to the phone rock. Like Ralph in *Lord of the Flies*, I had the conch. There were several missed calls from CBC. A complaint had been made to the CBC ombudsman demanding that I be terminated.

The CBC had put together a crisis team and wanted me to make an apology. I reminded them that I didn't work for the CBC. Yes, *22 Minutes* aired on the CBC, but I was not an employee. I also had not yet signed a contract for the next season of the show. They were making vague threats to fire someone who didn't work for them. I then reminded them that CBC had aired a sketch from their flagship show *The Rick Mercer Report* in which Rick appeared as a greasy TV pitchman hocking "The Miracle Panic Closet Organizer." A Stephen Harper look-alike was curled up in a ball at the bottom of a cluttered closet. "Hang your shirts, store your hats, hide your prime minister," Rick said. "Other closet organizers would have Stephen in a fetal position on top of your shoes, possibly ruining them. Not with the Miracle Closet Organizer. The shoes go on top of the prime minister."

Yes, I argued, I had posted a picture of myself in Harper's closet, but you guys put out a casting call for a Harper look-alike and built a closet.

Eventually things calmed down and the news cycle moved on, as it always does. In hindsight, I guess there is a reason I was initially so flippant about Mr. Harper and his closet. To explain, I have to tell you about my friend Curtis Barrett.

~

Curtis is a Mountie from Newfoundland and Labrador. On the day of the shooting, Curtis was working on Parliament Hill screening vehicles for explosives. When he heard about the gunshots fired in Centre Block, he ran in through the front door. He, with three other officers, walked down the Hall of Honour towards the Library of Parliament. Curtis and the others distracted Zehaf-Bibeau. This enabled Sergeant-at-Arms Kevin Vickers to jump from his hiding spot, shooting at Zehaf-Bibeau as he fell to the floor. Curtis fired as well, approaching the gunman as he did so. Barrett shot fifteen times. His final bullet landed in Zehaf-Bibeau's head.

Vickers went to the closet, telling Prime Minister Harper that he had "put him down." Curtis went off to guard the NDP caucus, believing there to be another shooter in the building. He stayed there for six hours with his gun drawn.

Vickers was hailed as a hero. He was made Canada's ambassador to Ireland. And Curtis? He was ignored. The official report says that both Vickers and Barrett "fired their weapons and neutralized the threat." But you've probably only heard of Kevin Vickers's heroism that day. That's because, as a senior RCMP officer told Curtis, "The Vickers train has left the station." The media already had their hero. The history books had been written, and Curtis's name would not be found inside.

Nobody checked on him. Nobody followed up. Nobody honoured him. Meanwhile, his mental health deteriorated. Curtis suffered his PTSD in silence while he watched news report after news report claiming that Kevin Vickers was a hero and the RCMP had failed at their job. Curtis became so broken-hearted that one day he broke his TV. His relationship ended. A year later, the RCMP's Health Services division told him that they didn't have any record of him being involved in any shooting. It was as if he didn't exist at all.

Eventually he did get the help he needed. Recognition came when Governor General David Johnston presented him with the Star of Courage, Canada's second-highest award for bravery. But Curtis didn't want medals. He just wanted to be believed. He told me how much pain those news reports caused him. The report that broke the story, by my dear friend Evan Solomon of CTV, weighed especially heavy on him. Curtis felt that the chance to speak to Evan and tell his side of the story would give him some closure for that part of his journey.

I got in touch with Evan, and because he is a thoughtful and wonderful person, he agreed to meet with Curtis. We had dinner together in Ottawa, and Curtis and Evan got to share their sides of what happened. It was a beautiful thing to see. Evan listened intently, and the two of them came away from it as friends. Evan even invited Curtis to be his guest at the Parliamentary Press Gallery dinner that year, where I was able to introduce Curtis to Prime Minister Trudeau. Trudeau thanked him for his service. A different prime minister should have done that on the day of the shooting, but I was delighted to see a prime minister finally give him the acknowledgment he deserved.

These days, Curtis is a hero of a different kind. Yes, he's still a bomb technician, but he also speaks to those who suffer from PTSD. He bravely shares his story of survival and goes to help wherever he is needed. I once shared the stage with him as he spoke to a ballroom of first-responders and veterans. I saw first hand the healing effect his story had on them. Curtis is a hero for what he did on October 22, 2014. But to me, he's a bigger hero for what he has done every day since. He's a great husband, a wonderful dad and a loyal and supportive friend.

Do I regret posting the picture in the closet? Yes. In comedy, timing is everything, and there really is no time for making fun of anything about that dreadful day. Maybe, to quote my friend Michelle, I was a "f**king embarrassment." But I think the way Curtis Barrett was treated is an even bigger f**king embarrassment. I truly wish some of these politicians had cared as much about the Mountie who suffered alone as they did about a picture of me in a closet.

14

FROM THE BASEMENT
TO THE ROOF

AFTER ALL MY YEARS spent criss-crossing the country and checking in on our international affairs, people often ask me what is the most interesting place I've been. I can't pick one because there are two that are equally fascinating, both for their location and for the madcap journeys that led me to them.

I didn't expect to end up in either. The unknown has been good to me. The best thing you can do when chasing a story is to let it lead you. Sticking to a failing plan leads to failure. "Rolling with it" has never failed me, but it has made me quite dizzy.

In 2010, we applied for and gained entry to a time-honoured tradition in the United States—the pardoning of the Thanksgiving turkey. The president holds a brief ceremony at the Rose Garden of the White House where he is presented with two turkeys, which he spares the indignity of becoming a Thanksgiving dinner. These are not to be confused with all of the turkeys that allowed former president Trump to gain access to the White House in the first place and who he pardoned on his way out the door.

I was filled with excitement as I walked up the driveway of 1600 Pennsylvania Avenue for the first time. I couldn't help but reflect on the history that surrounded me. This was the very same place that Canucks burned to the ground during the War of 1812. This was where

General Zod made the president kneel in *Superman II*, and the site of the alien invasion in *Independence Day*. History was all around us.

We entered the James S. Brady Press Briefing Room and took our seats. The iconic room seemed much smaller in real life. It was built by Richard Nixon in 1969 to cover over the pool where his rival Kennedy had loved to entertain "guests." The guests were always ladies and they somehow managed to stop by only when Mrs. Kennedy was out of town. I wandered up to the famous podium flanked by white columns and took in the moment. My father had worked all his life as a newsman for a radio station in St. John's and now here I was at the White House with the Presidential Seal behind me.

"Get away from that podium!" a voice bellowed from across the room. A grey-haired man with a necklace of laminated security passes around his neck shooed me away from the coveted position. He paused for a moment as if he recognized me. But that couldn't be possible. I was a Canadian entertainer in America. I was basically invisible.

"You," he said, pointing at me with a concerned look. "You better not mess up this press conference."

"Me?" I said, trying to figure out how he could be figuring me out. "I'm just a reporter from Canada, eh?"

"Oh, I know who you are," he said, raising his pants to reveal a maple leaf tattoo on his shin. "You're that comedian. My mother is Canadian. We have a cottage up there and the only station we can get is the CBC. I know you."

I started to gather my things, hoping security wouldn't do much probing. "Don't worry," he said, sitting down in one of the famous rows of blue press seats. "I won't turn you in. My mother would kill me." I had been saved by a lack of cable. Thank god his mother was cheap.

"Hey," he said, jumping to his feet. "Do you want to see the basement?" Did I want to see the basement of the White House? That would be a yes. "I'm not really supposed to do this, but what the hell. In a minute I'm going to walk up behind the podium and open a door. When I do, you just follow right after me. Okay?"

I couldn't help thinking that this might be some kind of elaborate ruse to get me tased. He walked over to the door with purpose and opened it. We descended some steps to a room filled with cables and what looked like computer servers. The walls were covered in tiles.

"This is the old pool," he explained. "It's like a natural bunker, so they keep the servers here. These tiles are the original pool tiles. They just covered over Kennedy's pool. Didn't change a thing. Now they can't. It's a historic site so they're not allowed to."

From what I could tell, the podium where the press secretary speaks is at the deep end, which makes perfect sense, as most people in that role are usually in over their head. The tiles were covered in names written in marker.

"What's with the graffiti?" I asked.

"Sometimes, they bring VIPs down here when they have a party. They let them sign the tiles." Everywhere I looked there was a famous name. Sugar Ray Leonard. Laura Bush. Anderson Cooper. Tom Hanks. Bono. "Here," he said, passing me a Sharpie. "You should sign, too. My mom thinks you're a celebrity." That was both one of the kindest gestures anyone has ever offered me and one of the most backhanded compliments I have ever received.

When I finished signing he said, "They can't ever take that tile down, so that'll be there long after you're dead. I'll be retiring soon, so screw it." I felt the weight of that sentence in my mind. Someday, hundreds of years into the future, an archeologist might well be brushing a layer of dust off that very tile. They would photograph it, upload it into some futuristic device and wonder, "Mark Critch? Who the hell is that?" Of course, someone looking at that tile today would probably wonder the very same thing.

I am often amazed at the situations I find myself in and the places they lead me to, but I am never surprised by the kindness of strangers.

~

There's no telling where the current will take you if you just give in and say yes. I was shooting a piece on Parliament Hill in 2014 with an MP who shall remain nameless. He was well known for having an open-door policy. There was also an open-bottle policy and people from all parties would gather in his office for drinks. Ice would be broken, deals would be made, arguments would be had, fights would break out, and then everybody would make up over a beer or six.

After an interview one night, my cameraman Pete, our field producer Cory and I were sitting in his office enjoying a drink when his eyes lit up with excitement. "Have you ever been up in the Peace Tower?" he asked.

I had been all over Parliament Hill in my career but I wasn't exactly sure of the geography. "I think so. I mean, I guess so. Which offices are in that part?"

"No, no," he said, waving his arms at me. "I mean the very top. Have you ever stuck your head out of the top of the Peace Tower and touched the flagpole?" That I had not done. "Well then, we gotta do it!" he said emphatically, and opened another beer.

"Sure," I said with a yawn. "If you can line it up, we should do it sometime."

"Not sometime. Now!" It was around ten o'clock at night. Pete and Cory looked at me with a shrug. We were not going to get this offer again. How could we say no?

"I know a guy with a key!" the MP exclaimed, picking up his phone. We were soon met by a custodian holding a ring with more keys than a Celine Dion solo. We rode an elevator to a floor I didn't know existed. We were directly behind one of the clock faces of the Peace Tower. The huge white disc in front of us looked as big as the moon. This would have been more than enough to make my night, but it turned out we still had a climb ahead of us.

"The elevator only goes this far. We have to take the stairs after this." We climbed up the white metal stairs that reminded me of ones I had climbed in lighthouses back home. They were dusty and creaked slightly as I made my way up. Or perhaps that sound came from the MP as he huffed his way up ahead of me. The higher we went, the more threadbare the cloak of invulnerability lent to me by the liquor. I was excited, but I still couldn't shake the feeling that I really shouldn't be doing this. Sobriety would not be my friend. I needed the bravado only afforded by booze.

"You sure this is okay?" I asked.

"Absolutely," he called back to me as his butt wriggled up the stairs just inches from my face. "As a member of Parliament I have the right to go wherever I want."

I locked eyes with the custodian. "Is that right?" I asked.

"I guess so," he said with a shrug. Something inside me was telling me that I was going to get arrested.

These stairs led to a door and beyond that another set of stairs that were so steep they bordered on being a ladder.

"One at a time here," the MP bellowed. The custodian pushed upon a hatch and there we were, at the top of the Peace Tower, in a tiny white room with the kind of windows you might expect someone to shoot arrows through at a rival king's army. Like Kennedy's pool, the walls inside were covered with signatures. I gladly signed my name there too.

The custodian unlocked the hatch and I climbed up a stepladder to come face to face with the flagpole that stands some ninety-eight metres above the Ottawa skyline. The Canadian flag flapped above me in the breeze, and for a moment I felt like Neil Armstrong. *One small step for a drunk. One giant step for drunk kind.*

"You sure this isn't going to set off any alarms?" I asked. Everyone had a little think. No answer came.

"Uh, guys," came a worried voice from the room below.

"Everything okay?" I asked.

The custodian pointed at the elevator doors. "The elevator's moving."

"Oh," I said. "Is that bad?"

"It shouldn't be moving," he said. "I've got the key."

"Well, if you've got the key then who's in the elevator?" I already knew the answer.

We all stood in silence waiting for the elevator doors to open. The MP stepped to the front as if he was going to shield us from something and, realizing that this was all his fault, I tucked in behind him.

Three officers stepped out of the elevator. I half-jokingly shouted, "Don't shoot. I'm a clown." They looked at us the way a disappointed parent looks at a child after they've been found trying to sneak in through their bedroom window after a night drinking. They insisted that we get back in the elevator and get the hell out of there. It was the quietest elevator ride I had ever taken. I was beginning to wonder if I would ever be allowed onto Parliament Hill again.

Finally, one of the officers spoke. "You're from Newfoundland, right?" By his accent, I could tell that he was French-Canadian.

"I am," I said.

This caused him to let out a heavy sigh. "Have you ever been to the Memorial Chamber?" he asked, in a way that made me think he was hoping I had. The Memorial Chamber is a solemn marble room in the Peace Tower. It is dedicated to all Canadians who have died in war. Stained glass windows encircle the space and filter light that shines down on seven altars made of stone and bronze. Each altar holds a different Book of Remembrance that contain the names of the more than 118,000 Canadians who have died fighting in various conflicts.

"No. I have never been to the Memorial Chamber," I said like a man on death row being offered a last meal.

"Did you know that Newfoundland has its own Book of Remembrance there?"

I did. Newfoundland joined Canada in 1949, so they had to add a book just for us.

"Did you have any family members who served?"

"Yes. J.J. Tobin. He died in the First World War," I told him. The First World War was hard on the Dominion of Newfoundland. From a total population of 240,000, nearly twelve thousand men would volunteer for service. On the first day of the Battle of the Somme, July 1, 1916, eight hundred soldiers of the Newfoundland Regiment waded into the trenches at the Battle of Beaumont-Hamel. Only sixty-eight would answer roll call the next day. July 1 is Canada Day for most of the country. In Newfoundland, however, it is still Memorial Day. The regiment fought so bravely that it was the only unit of the British Army to earn the designation "Royal" during the war.

The weight of that day's loss touched almost every Newfoundland family. I told the Mountie that I never knew of my connection until I made a pilgrimage to the site of that battle with my friend the actor Allan Hawco. On our way there, we discovered not only that we had ancestors who knew each other, but that they had signed up and sailed to Europe together. And not only did they die side by side, but they were buried side by side—a fact we learned when we visited their graves at Marcoing, France.

That story did it for my Mountie captor. He let loose a much longer sigh. "You can't leave without seeing that. Come on." He pressed the button for the floor of the Memorial Chamber.

He unlocked the heavy iron gate and led us into the room. The floor was made of stone collected from the battlefields of Europe, and our footsteps echoed as we filed in. He pointed out the altar on which the Newfoundland Book of Remembrance rested.

"They turn a page in the book every day at eleven o'clock. I'll give you some time to pay your respects."

I stood there in silence, moved by the beauty of the room and the weight of all it represented. I thought of all those young men in the Newfoundland Regiment slaughtered in the Battle of Beaumont-Hamel. I wondered what they would think if they had known that the flag they were fighting under, the Red Ensign of the Dominion of Newfoundland, no longer existed. Or that they were now remembered in a book in a hall of what had been a foreign country to them.

My moment of silence stretched to two moments to a minute to a good ten minutes as I avoided a possible arrest. Finally the cop said, "Okay. I think that's enough."

We carried on in silence to the lobby, where notes were taken, phone calls were made and we were sternly reprimanded. Then we were told we had to leave. I shamefully made my way down through the Rotunda and paused for a moment to turn back to the officer.

"I have to say," I said truthfully, "that was the nicest way I have ever been kicked out of a place in my life. It was very . . . Canadian."

As I walked out into the winter night, I looked up at the flag flapping contentedly in the breeze as thick Ottawa snowflakes began to lazily fall and melt in the heat of the Centennial Flame.

If someone asks me where the most interesting place I've been is, I'll tell them it's a tie. My career has taken me from the basement of the White House to the roof of the Peace Tower. I will always remember those as my favourites, as much for the places themselves as for the unexpected journeys to get there.

15

SLEEVEENS

I AM NON-PARTISAN. ONE THING that more than twenty years of satirizing politicians has taught me is that all political parties are equally ridiculous. They all have liars, charlatans and narcissists. They also have kind-hearted, hard-working people who are genuinely concerned with the well-being of their fellow Canadians. But those ones usually get voted out. The strange thing about spending this much time around politicians is that it seems to make you trust them less but like them more.

When I was growing up, politics was the only sport we ever watched in my house. My parents provided a running commentary as we watched the evening news just like it was *Coach's Corner*.

TV NEWS ANCHOR: The minister said today that the investment—
DAD: He stole a watch at Ayre's in the mall.
TV NEWS ANCHOR:—will be one that his constituents will be seeing—
MOM: Yes-my-god-he-left-his-wife-for-her-sister! I-know-cuz-a-girl-that-works-in-his-office-gets-her-hair-done-with-a-girl-that's-running-around-with-his-wife's-sister's-brother.
DAD: That's just gossip, Mary.
TV NEWS ANCHOR:—for years to come. The minister said it would be his last announcement, however, as he would be leaving public life before the next election.

DAD: I heard he passed a bad cheque at Bowring's so they made him resign.

Neither of my parents was overly fond of politicians, but my father did have a professional respect for them. My mother offered no such courtesy. She said they were all sleeveens. "Sleeveen" is a great word. It's from the Irish Gaelic and it means " a smooth-tongued rogue." The very essence of politics is "sleevenry."

Politicians are human, after all, and being such they are subject to the same frailties that we all are. That has been painfully evident to me over the years. A new party leader is at first worshipped almost like a god. Four years later, the very same people who once carried a leader's name on a banner probably wouldn't cross the street to spit on them.

I once worried that I wouldn't last two weeks in my job, but as the years passed, I found myself outlasting many of the politicians I had covered. Then I outlasted their replacements. I have learned that the ones who are comfortable in their own skin generally have the best time of it.

Jean Chrétien was like that. Sometimes you didn't even need an appointment to see the prime minister. If you were on the Hill, it was always worth checking if the big guy was around. More often than not, he would shout from the inner office, "The Newfie is here? What do they want me to do? I could choke him?"

He once told me, on-camera, "A lot of people will agree with you today, but I cannot say that I agree to do with you today." I turned to the camera and said, "Now that's a Chrétien quote! I have no idea what he said and if you put that on paper no one would ever know what he said. He is perfect for politics."

Chrétien loved to choke people for a laugh. It became known as the Shawinigan Handshake. Shawinigan was Chrétien's hometown, and the "handshake" refers to the chokehold he gave to anti-poverty pro-testor Bill Clennett in 1996 in Hull, Quebec. When Clennett blocked the prime minister's way, Chrétien grabbed him by the neck and forced him to the ground, breaking one of Clennett's teeth. Chrétien always acted as his own best security. When he woke to find a knife-wielding intruder in his residence in 1995, he grabbed an Inuit carving to protect himself.

I only ever saw the master showman on his heels once. In 2005, I went to a session of the Gomery Commission inquiry into the mishandling of millions of dollars as part of the Liberals' sponsorship program. Chrétien was called to the stand and was unapologetic, claiming it had all been necessary to protect federalism in Quebec after the 1995 referendum. The inquiry had heard that the Prime Minister's Office had emblazoned three hundred golf balls with Chrétien's signature at a cost of four dollars each. Justice John Gomery called the whole business "small-town cheap."

Was Chrétien classy for using taxpayers' money to brand golf balls to impress cronies? No. Did it work? Yes. If Chrétien had emblazoned his name on hockey pucks, then yes, that would be "small-town cheap." This was "big-city cheap."

I figured out which door Chrétien would enter through to avoid the press and waited. He shot through the hallway, swinging a briefcase with the determination of a man who did not want to answer questions. He stopped, surprised to see me. I told him, "I think you're one hundred percent innocent of all charges. But the word's not really getting out. Do you think, maybe, you should hire an ad agency to help raise your profile?"

"I'd certainly not hire you," he shot back.

I held up a red Sharpie and a golf ball and asked him if he would sign it for me. He looked confused for a moment, then took the marker and signed his name on my forehead. Then he turned on his heel and headed off to take the stand. Something had rattled him, and I couldn't figure out what it was.

When I watched his testimony, I saw that the briefcase he was carrying was filled with golf balls. Each one had been signed by someone famous, including some American presidents. George W. Bush, Bill Clinton and Vice-President Al Gore had all put their names on golf balls. Chrétien asked Judge Gomery if he thought that they, too, were "small-town cheap."

In a parting shot, Chrétien's final ball was from the law firm that then employed former prime minister Brian Mulroney, Gomery Commission counsel Bernard Roy and Judge Gomery's own daughter. Do not mess with Chrétien.

There was no stopping him. He appeared on our show after quadruple bypass surgery and I gave him a gift: his own defibrillator. He celebrated his eightieth birthday on *22 Minutes* and we looked back at his career. I had PhotoShopped him into historic photos to appear alongside some famous Canadians from the country's past.

"Now, I don't want to say you're old," I said, holding up a photo of Chrétien at Louis Riel's trial, "but here you are defending Louis Riel." I then showed a photo of Chrétien in the crowd watching as the last spike was hammered into the Canadian Pacific Railway track. Finally, I showed a picture of him attending the Charlottetown Conference to discuss Confederation in 1864.

"You know," he joked, "George-Étienne Cartier was sick, so I replaced him."

I gave him a cake with eighty lit candles on it. Peter Mansbridge came by with a fire extinguisher to help snuff out the flames. But one wasn't needed. Chrétien blew them all out with one puff, like the Big Bad Wolf he was. And then, of course, he choked me.

~

Jack Layton never met a camera he didn't like either. Not only was the leader of the NDP always available for an interview, but he usually brought his guitar. Layton was the true stereotype of a Dipper—a moustachioed bicycle-riding folk singer. Once when he joined me on the show, I started to make fun of his repetitive catchphrases. I brought out a couple of beers to play the Jack Layton Drinking Game. The rules were that we had to take a drink whenever he said "making Parliament work," "kitchen table" or "working families."

Without skipping a beat Layton said, "What we're concerned about is getting some help for working families who right now are sitting around the kitchen table hoping to make Parliament work and they can't afford a beer and that's wrong." We knocked back three pints and we were on our way.

I once went to Parliament Hill dressed as Santa Claus to ask the party leaders what they wanted for Christmas. Jack asked Santa for some keys.

"Some keys?" I repeated, confused.

"To 24 Sussex," he said, with a smile.

"Oh well," I said, shaking my head. "You're going to be a very disappointed little boy, Jack."

But with each election, support grew a little more and Jack got a little closer to getting those keys. In 2011, his party did the impossible and won enough seats to become Canada's Official Opposition. By then he was battling prostate cancer, though, and that was one of the few fights he wouldn't win. The last message he had for Canadians was, "Love is better than anger. Hope is better than fear. Optimism is better than despair."

His words were so moving that Joe Biden stole them for a speech at the Democratic National Convention. Jack would have loved that.

Jack Layton was irreplaceable as party leader. I covered the NDP convention where the party tried to do the impossible. On the convention floor, I managed to get interviews with every candidate except the eventual winner, Tom Mulcair. He didn't want anything to do with us. If I lost the NDP, who was I going to get to talk to me when nobody else would?

I stood by the steps that led to the news desk where Peter Mansbridge was waiting to interview the newly crowned leader. As Mulcair approached, I tried to plead my case again with his staffer. We really wanted an interview. "I'm sorry," he told me. There was no use, it would not happen. So I told Pete to fire up his camera and I started to speak loud enough for everyone to hear.

"That's it for us," I began. "Thomas Mulcair is the next leader of the New Democratic Party and the only candidate who has refused to talk to us. Jack Layton was never afraid to talk. But I'm here to tell you, dear viewers, that Tom Mulcair is no Jack Layton. Good night."

The staffer hurried over to me. "You can't say that," he said.

"Just did," I said, rolling up my microphone cord. "And just as many people watch us as watch him," I said, pointing to the back of Peter Mansbridge's shiny but impressive head.

"Wait here a minute," he said, and ran off in Mulcair's direction. Within moments I was being introduced to the new leader of the NDP and his wife. I produced a bottle of Orange Crush (the media had dubbed the NDP's recent success an Orange Crush) and two champagne flutes. We toasted his win and I welcomed him to the show. I wanted him to get my scent and hopefully he would see, in the coming years, that I wasn't so bad.

When he rolled out an affordable childcare plan, I invited Tom to meet me at a daycare. "Hey, kids," I said to the children there, "do you know who this is?"

"Santa!" they enthusiastically replied. Mulcair took softball questions from the children. I had rehearsed one little girl to hit him with something harder.

"Didn't Paul Martin's Liberals try to reform child care in 2005, but the NDP voted against it?" she asked. Tom was speechless for a moment, before breaking into a huge laugh. In politics, it's always better to laugh than to answer the question.

I was shocked when Mulcair joined me in the pit filled with multicoloured balls and let the kids jump on him.

"Hey, kids," I shouted. "Now's your chance to see if it's a real beard!" The kids bounced on Tom and tugged his beard but he just smiled. And when the camera was turned off, he was still smiling. Was this the same guy?

I began to play him in sketches, and when I was wearing a beard and an orange tie, I looked enough like him to make it work. I asked Tom if I could interview him *as* him. He agreed and I found myself at Stornoway, the official residence of the leader of the Opposition, at a time when there was a real chance that he would become our next prime minister.

"Tom," I began, "you say there will be a balanced budget."

"Yes, there will be," he answered.

"This is the NDP," I replied. "What the hell are you talking about?"

"It's our NDP," he countered. "Tommy Douglas. Seventeen balanced budgets in a row and he brought in medicare."

"I thought we'll finally form a government," I complained. "We'll have a big drum circle and everybody gets a bike. We're going to have some fun and you're going to balance the budget. You're too far right for me and I'm you! Where is my NDP! You lost my vote!"

When we were finished, Mulcair and his team had to rush off to give a speech in Quebec. They turned to us, apologetically, and said, "We have to go. Can you let yourself out when you're done?" Tom trusted people. I immediately abused that trust and ran upstairs to see what his private bathroom looked like and took a picture with the official toilet of the leader of the Opposition.

Tom's hopes of moving from Stornoway to 24 Sussex were soon dashed. On election night in 2015 I was at NDP headquarters for *22 Minutes* and the CBC coverage. Trudeau's Liberals swept the map that night. I have not since been in a room that glum. I appeared in a live TV-hit for the CBC's election coverage that night, hosted by Peter Mansbridge.

"It's a bloodbath," I began from the near-empty convention room. "Do I know how to pick a party! I can't hear you over the sobbing, Peter." Mulcair seemed to disappear after that loss. There were no interviews, no speeches. He had gone off the map. Everyone from the CBC's Rosie Barton to the *National Post* was asking, "Where is Tom Mulcair?"

I had an idea. Drake's song "Hotline Bling" was burning up the charts and the video of him dancing alone in an oddly shaped room was everywhere. What if the answer to "Where is Tom?" wasn't that he was heartbroken at the colossal loss? What if it was, "He's just chilling and dancing to 'Hotline Bling'?"

The chance of him doing it was small. The chance of him knowing what "Hotline Bling" was, was microscopic. My right hand, producer Cory Gibson, got in touch with Tom's right hand, George Smith, and explained our idea. George ran it by Tom, explaining and re-explaining what "Hotline Bling" was, and eventually we got an answer. Tom was in. We picked up some Drake-ish clothing and met them at a studio.

When they arrived, I watched as George patiently taught Tom Mulcair how to bop up and down in a crouching position like Drake. We shot two parts, one in which Tom danced all alone and another where I joined him. Tom was all smiles, and it seemed like this bit of silliness was just what the doctor ordered for someone who had just lost an election.

The scene became an instant smash and was soon almost as popular in Canada as the original Drake video. The *Huffington Post* proclaimed, "Thomas Mulcair Did Drake's 'Hotline Bling.' It Was Everything."

The last interview I did with Tom was after his leadership review, when 52 percent of delegates said they wanted a new leader. That same year, he had won *Maclean's* magazine's Parliamentarian of the Year award. Ottawa can be a tough town. I asked Tom to join me at the Centennial Flame on Parliament Hill for a weenie roast. We sat next to the fire, roasting hotdogs on sticks and enjoying a couple of beers that we kept cold in a snowbank.

If you had told me on the night Thomas Mulcair became leader of the NDP that one day I would be roasting weenies in the Centennial Flame with him, I would never have believed you. As people passed us, they all shouted their congratulations to him. The cops on the Hill just shook their heads and laughed at us. It was a nice send-off for a nice man.

~

Sometimes I am accused of favouring the left over the right. I don't. At different times in my life I have voted for all three of the major political parties. That's because the more politicians I get to know, the more faith I have in individuals over parties. If I don't interview as many Conservatives as I do Dippers or Liberals, it isn't for lack of trying. In my experience, Conservatives are generally much tougher to get a hold of. People on the right love to call leftists "snowflakes," but if you ask me, it's Conservative politicians who generally can't take a joke.

It also doesn't help that they usually dislike the CBC in general. Their current leader, Erin O'Toole, even campaigned on dismantling it. I remember once being in the Toronto office of the late Jim Flaherty when he was the finance minister in the Harper government. He invited me to stick around and have a drink once the interview was complete. We started to chat about Ireland and music and a host of other things that were apolitical. Jim paused as he stared out the window, fixated on his view of the big exploding-pizza logo of the CBC, high atop the corporation's headquarters on John Street.

"You know," he said wistfully, "every time I see that building I think, There's a billion dollars I could cut right there."

"Forget who you were talking to for a second?" I asked.

"Yes," he said, and took another sip of his drink. "Yes, I did."

When Andrew Scheer became leader of the Conservative Party in 2015, I had hopes of a reset. He was younger than I was and he was a huge *Simpsons* fan. Surely he would be able to take a joke. I visited his office to meet him for the first time. I had been there before with Tom Mulcair and Michael Ignatieff. The Office of the Leader of the Opposition is the most beautiful office on the Hill. It's designed in a mid-seventeenth-century style. Oak woodwork frames walls decorated with frescoes showing scenes of medieval knights.

Each new leader I interviewed there delighted in showing me the same feature, a secret door hidden inside a carved oak panel next to the fireplace. It was installed by Mackenzie King to provide an escape route away from unwanted visitors. I never had the heart to tell them that I already knew. The only thing different about the office when Scheer showed it to me was a rather large crucifix over the television. Scheer is a devout Catholic.

Perhaps that was why he refused to walk in Pride parades. When he was running against Trudeau in 2019, I decided to bring the parade to him. Scheer was speaking in a strip mall in Halifax. His team of worker bees had told us that he would not have time for me, so we just showed up at his rally unannounced. I brought three of the show's writers with me and planted them around the room with the Conservative faithful to pose as supporters. Under their coats, they were wearing rainbow shirts that said things like "Fyne Minister" and "Sashay Away from Debt." When the time came, I was going to give Andrew Scheer a flash mob Pride march.

The worker bees buzzed around me as soon as I entered the room. I slowly made my way to the front as some of the people in the crowd heckled me.

"Kick him out!" someone shouted. "He's fake news!" Yes. I was. I couldn't argue with him.

"Don't talk to him!" someone else shouted. "CBC lies!"

I would say my cover had been blown if I wasn't holding a mic flag that said "22 Minutes" on it. The crowd began to jostle around me, forming a grey-haired wall between me and the stage. A man wearing a Trump button shouted, "Liberal hack!"

Scheer walked out to a huge cheer. He spotted me and waved. I smiled back and beckoned him over. "Uh-oh," he said. "I see Mark Critch is here."

Surprisingly, Scheer defended me. "That's not true," he said, hushing the crowd. "Mark is my friend. I've spoken with him many times. We chatted about *The Simpsons*. It was fun."

"No!" the Trump fan shouted in disbelief.

Andrew told me he would be over to talk to me after his speech. I was conflicted. Scheer had defended me. Stephen Harper would have had me hauled out of there and the crowd would have cheered him for it. But Andrew was willing to come down and talk to me. It was my job to give as hard as I could, but in that moment I couldn't help but feel bad for doing it.

Scheer came over to me as his staffers pushed my writers to the foreground, in front of the hecklers. They were young. Little did they know what was about to happen.

I thanked Scheer for having my back, then I stabbed him in his.

"A lot of people have asked you to march in Pride parades," I began. "So I brought a Pride march to you." With that, the writers ripped open their coats to show their shirts. They threw glitter in the air. One held up a sign that read "We're here. We're Scheer. Get used to it."

"Sur-pride!" I yelled as they threw their arms around Andrew and jumped up and down behind him. "So now," I said, "you have at least one photo of you marching in a Pride parade, so that's off the list."

We ran out of the room as the guy with the Trump button pointed at us, screaming at no one in particular, "See? I told you! He can't be trusted!"

Maybe he had a point after all.

~

My best relationship with any politician was with the former premier of Newfoundland and Labrador, Danny Williams. He first caught my attention when he fought with Prime Minister Paul Martin over a campaign promise Martin had made to let Newfoundland and Labrador keep 100 percent of its offshore oil revenues. After Martin took office, he convened a first ministers' conference where he proposed an expenditure cap. Danny walked out of the room.

In Danny, I saw a politician who got who he was and wasn't afraid to make fun of it. This was rare. I loved it when he was in the national news because it meant that I was guaranteed to get a great piece out of the headline. Luckily, he was rarely out of the headlines.

In a controversial negotiating posture around the offshore revenue agreement, Danny later ordered the removal of all Canadian flags from provincial government buildings. A month later, the province struck a deal with Ottawa on the offshore oil issue and the flags started flying again. This win did not mark the end of his struggles with Ottawa. If he disliked Martin, he truly despised Harper.

When Harper's Conservative government reneged on an election pledge to exclude non-renewable energy sources from the provincial equalization formula, Williams launched the "ABC" campaign, telling Newfoundlanders and Labradorians to vote "Anything but Conservative." It made it impossible for the federal party to find candidates, and the Conservative Party still hasn't recovered in Newfoundland and Labrador.

I started to play Williams in sketches and portrayed him more as a Castro or Kim Jong Il type character than he was. One script featured me as Danny informing Prime Minister Harper that Newfoundland had developed a nuclear weapon. "The world will end at 8 p.m.," Danny warned, "8:30 in Newfoundland."

Williams appeared on the show many times over the years. But in 2010, he announced he was stepping down as premier. I'm sure some people wondered if he was quitting so he could focus more time on *22 Minutes*. At the time, I happened to be flying home to shoot a piece with iconic Canadian actor Gordon Pinsent. We were going to ride a float together in the St. John's Christmas Parade in a bit for our holiday special. I had heard the news about Williams as I was preparing to leave and was as shocked as anyone. Danny agreed to give us some time to shoot something, but the question was what to shoot.

The fact that I would have Newfoundland's favourite son in town when the premier stepped down meant I had to use Gordon. A plan started to formulate in my head. I asked Gordon if he owned a tuxedo and he said, "Of course." Dumb question. Next I called my friend Allan Hawco. His St. John's-shot series *Republic of Doyle* had just started to air. Maybe I could use Newfoundland's favourite PI in the skit?

I ordered a drink on the plane and wrote out a sketch on napkins. It began with me confronting the premier in a suite at the local Delta. I inform Williams that he cannot step down without asking the permission of the Supreme Newfoundlander, the Codfather. The Codfather was played by Gordon Pinsent.

GORDON: Well, did you get everything I asked? Did you get the oil?
DANNY: Yes, Codfather.
GORDON: Did you get the Lower Churchill?
DANNY: Yes, Codfather.
GORDON: Did you throw a tantrum, like a huge baby, every time you didn't get your way?

DANNY: Oh, yeah.

MARK: Yeah, he did that.

GORDON: Well then, by the power invested in me as Supreme New-foundlander and Canadian Icon Gordon Pinsent, I release you.

I then pulled a gun on the sitting premier of my home province and held him hostage, thinking that if I could find a way to keep him in the fray, I wouldn't have to learn a new impression. The scene ends with Danny being saved by the stars of *Republic of Doyle*—as they hold me back, Gordon Pinsent pummels me. All in all, it was a good day's work.

That night, the cast (minus Danny) and our crew went to a restaurant where Gordon regaled us with a lifetime of amazing stories, each one better than the last. We drank Scotch after Scotch, each one a bigger mistake than the last.

The next morning came early, and I found myself doing what I had initially come to do: appear on a float in a Christmas parade with Gordon Pinsent. I don't know whether you've ever been hungover in a parade before, but it's not a good idea. There was an actual marching band behind us, and every hit on the glockenspiel reverberated inside my booze-soaked skull like a church bell. While my unsettled stomach became queasier as the float we were on slowly crawled down the street, eighty-year-old Gordon was chipper and spry, delighting those young and old with every wave from King Babar's hand.

When we finally stopped, Gordon turned to me and said, "I'm getting a bit cold. Is there a ride to get me back to my hotel?" There should have been but there wasn't. All of our production vehicles and drivers were back where the parade had started. My hungover mind hadn't put any thought into the end of the parade. I was too busy concentrating on not puking.

The roads had been closed to traffic and were filling with the hundreds of spectators who had come out for the parade. It would have been impossible to get a cab in any reasonable amount of time, so I walked out into the street and flagged down the first car I saw. A

Honda Civic stopped for me. Inside, a tired mom was driving two exhausted children home. She rolled down the window.

"Hi," she said with a smile. "I know you! You were in the parade."

"That's right," I said, and pointed to Gordon. "And so was he. Would you mind dropping Mr. Pinsent at the Delta for me?" I asked without a hint of shame.

"I'd be honoured," she said. She turned to the child beside her. "Dustin! Get in the back seat! It's Mr. Pinsent."

I went back to get Gordon. "Your ride is here," I told him. "Thanks, buddy."

I held the door as Gordon slipped into the passenger seat, pulling a toy from under his bottom as he did so.

"Mr. Pinsent, what an honour to meet you," his driver shouted as Gordon took a moment to get his bearings. He looked back up at me with a concerned look as I shut the door. I tapped the roof and the car sped off down the road while Gordon looked back at me like a dog who'd thought he was going to the park but just realized he was being taken to the vet.

The piece we shot with Danny Williams went on to become one of the most loved skits in the show's history. Danny, like Chrétien, Peter MacKay, Tom Mulcair and others of all stripes, knew that people liked to see him get his lumps.

The best leaders are the ones who know who they are. They aren't afraid to say what they think. The ones who played along with me over the years did so because they weren't afraid to defend themselves. The ones who ran away? They weren't hiding from me. They were running from themselves.

One politician above all others has come to know the value of being able to take a joke. But it has taken some convincing. He has taught me to be nice to everyone on the way up, because you never know who will one day grow up to become prime minister.

16

JUSTIN TIME

'D ALWAYS BEEN SOMEWHAT intimidated whenever I interviewed a prime minister. I've interviewed Clark, Turner, Chrétien, Martin and Harper, but I only ever really got to know one prime minister. That is Justin Trudeau.

The BBC contacted me when he was first elected to the office. They knew I had interviewed him many times over the years and wanted to know how I thought he'd do. I predicted he would become his own opposition and fumble with some huge scandal of his own making. I told them that I thought he would bounce back, though. The one thing I had learned about Justin Trudeau over the years, I told them, was not to underestimate him.

It wasn't long before that prediction made me look like Nostradamus, because our prime minister had acted like a Nostra-dumbass.

In September of 2019, I was flying from Halifax to Vancouver to interview Green Party leader Elizabeth May. Leaders of parties that don't have a chance of forming government are always up for anything and make for great TV.

I was writing jokes on my laptop when my field producer, Cory Gibson, tapped me on the shoulder. "Did you get Wi-Fi on this flight yet?" he asked. I had not. Wi-Fi would mean I'd waste all of my writing time on Twitter arguing with accounts that had a pickup truck for a profile picture and names like YellowVester1867.

"Check the news," he said, before walking back up the aisle, shaking his head.

"Wait," I called after him. "What website?"

"Any of them," he said without looking back.

I logged on to see a video of Justin Trudeau holding a press conference on the prime minister's plane. "In 2001, when I was a teacher out in Vancouver, I attended an end-of-the-year gala where the theme was Arabian Nights. I dressed up," he continued, "in an Aladdin costume and put makeup on."

Makeup was an understatement. Trudeau admitted that he had worn brownface and then, because this is Canada, he had to admit it all over again *en français*. I looked around at the passengers around me. The picture was on every screen. There he was, dressed in an outfit that was basically straight off a Shriners' parade float. Makeup covered his face, but also his neck, his arms and his hands. This former drama teacher had really got into his role.

He was 29 years old at the time of the photo. Not 2 or 9, but 29. He was certainly old enough to know better. I could hear David Cochrane of CBC News shouting over the fray of reporters: "Is this the only time you've done something like that, Mr. Trudeau? Is that the only time?" *Of course it is, David*, I thought. *There's no way there's more than one picture of a Canadian prime minister in blackface!*

"When I was in high school," the PM said as he silently prayed for turbulence, "I dressed up at a talent show and sang 'Day-O' with makeup on." He repeated this in French and I learned that "Day-O" is the same in both of our official languages. "The fact of the matter is," Trudeau added, "that I've always—and you'll know this—been more enthusiastic about costumes than is sometimes appropriate." That was hardly a condemnation of the dangers of systemic racism.

I closed my browser, opened the Elizabeth May script I had been working on and deleted everything I had been writing. Nothing else mattered now.

Trudeau had apparently worn blackface more times than Al Jolson, and the story of the "woke" prime minister's face instantly became front-page news all over the world. The pundits all felt that this was something no politician could ever recover from. I wasn't so sure. Trudeau had surprised me more than once.

~

Justin Trudeau and I are roughly the same age, although he (despite being prettier) is three years older. I've watched him grow from a seed to a fully grown pot plant. At the time that Justin was enthusiastically covering even his knees and elbows in blackface, I was starting my job at *22 Minutes*. I was beginning my television career just as he was beginning to test the political waters to see if he could walk on them. He dipped his foot into those dangerous waters at about the same time that I dove head-first into the frigid puddle of Canadian comedy. I have watched, sometimes from afar and sometimes barely an inch from his face, as he rocketed to the heights of political power. Well, maybe not rocketed. There was a failure to launch followed by several accidental detonations, scrubbed takeoffs and re-entry problems.

As I got my footing in my career, Justin too found his place. As my confidence grew, his mushroomed at a pace not seen unless you put a Peep in the microwave. He was the first prime minister I covered who felt to me more like a peer than a world leader.

We first crossed paths at the Liberal leadership convention in 2003. Justin was thirty-two. At that point in his life, he was more known for what he wasn't doing than for what he had accomplished. He had not yet run for office, but he had been a teacher, an engineering student, a camp counsellor, a nightclub bouncer and a snowboard instructor. He'd gone through more professions than Barbie.

Liberal smugness emanated from deep within him, like the red glow that came from Rudolph's nose. Justin, with your future bright, won't you guide us past the right?

I walked up to the Dauphin and asked him for an interview. Loving the camera, even then, he flicked his lustrous mane like a champion show horse. A small group of fawning Liberals watched from the sidelines, praying that he would finally announce his intention to run and they could tell their grandchildren that they were there when the Word became flesh.

I asked him if he would run, but he was all "umms" and "ahhs." He reminded me of a newborn fawn, struggling to stand up on his feet for the first time. Politics is all about speaking at length without saying anything and, so far, he was doing a pretty good job.

"Come on," I encouraged him. "You've got to run. You're like the Julian Lennon of Canadian politics," I said, referring to his hand-me-down fame. That was the first time I saw Justin Trudeau bristle. His shoulders rolled back, his lower jaw slacked and his lips curled. His hands waved around as if he was juggling imaginary balls but somehow still dropping them. It was "Trudeau-esque."

He was not happy. But I didn't care. He was just the kid of a former PM, and, seeking bigger fish, I thanked him and left. I walked past the wall of Trudeau true believers who eyed me as if I was Judas fleeing the Last Supper with six pieces of silver in my hand.

Of course, Trudeau did run eventually. How could he not? His supporters said that the biggest thing going for him was the public's memory of his father. His detractors would say that was his biggest liability. Would Trudeaumania strike again, or did the country's previous exposure to that particular political pandemic make most Canadians immune?

In 2008, I watched curiously as Justin narrowly beat out a Bloc Québécois candidate to win a seat in the riding of Papineau, in Montreal. Right away, people started looking at him as a possible future prime minister. I, on the other hand, only looked at him as fodder for jokes. Justin Trudeau was good for business.

In 2010, Justin was growing a moustache for Movember, a charity event held every November to raise money to fight prostate cancer. We challenged each other over Twitter to a moustache-growing contest, with the winner to be revealed on our show. My Irish genetics gave me the beard of a kiwi, but I felt confident that I could out-stache a prime minister's son.

We met at a barbershop in Papineau. As we faced off, I told Trudeau, "I'm well on my way to a Burton Cummings, and you look more like the guy in grade nine who used to sell me hash." I poked at his moustache. "I mean, it's a little thin and a little creepy-looking. You look a little like a sex offender. Traditionally a hard sell with voters."

"You know what?" he said, grabbing a hot towel. "This has been bugging me all afternoon." Then he wiped my lip with it. I had darkened my light moustache with mascara to give myself the edge. It was the Movember version of the Ben Johnson Olympic doping scandal. I liked that he called me out. He wasn't afraid to have fun.

With Movember finished, I suggested he raise money for a truly hopeless cause—the Liberal Party of Canada. Things were not going well for Justin's party. I had been at the convention where Stéphane Dion was chosen as leader. The Québécois cameramen in the back of the room all burst into laughter when he was announced. I asked them what was so funny. "In Quebec," one of them told me, "the cartoons in the papers show him like a little mouse. He will never be prime minister." The Liberals would not have much more luck with their next few leaders.

Michael Ignatieff had spent less time in Canada than Wayne Gretzky. He had lived in the UK from 1978 to 2000 and loved to remind Canadians that he had taught at Harvard. Somehow Canadians didn't embrace a possible prime minister who couldn't be bothered to live in the country he hoped to run. Not only did the Liberals lose the election in 2011, but their new leader even lost his own seat. It was the worst showing in history for the Liberal Party.

Some people complain that Canadian politics is too inbred with elite insiders to effectively represent Canadians. Maybe they say that because the Liberals next picked Ignatieff's former university roommate, Bob Rae, to be their interim leader. The party needed a fresh face to take over for Iggy so they looked as far as the next bunk.

The leadership convention in 2012 was a small, dismal affair, more like a wake than a party. I reached out to all of the surviving Liberal MPs to film a sketch about their woes. We met at a table in a St-Hubert chicken restaurant over which I had strung a banner that read "Happy Birthday." I had crossed out "Birth" and replaced it with "Liberal," and punctuated the scene with a few sad, limp balloons.

Marc Garneau, John McCallum, Scott Brison, Dominic LeBlanc, Carolyn Bennett and the leader himself, Bob Rae, all squeezed into the booth. The only person who turned down our invitation was the one who loved the camera the most. Trudeau was a no-show. It seemed he didn't want to be seen at a table of "losers." Justin was up to something.

He knew that he had to shake the image of the cute rich kid. The fastest way to do that, it seemed, was to give someone the opportunity to knock the silver spoon right out of his mouth. And so, Trudeau challenged Conservative senator Patrick Brazeau to take part in a boxing match to raise money to fight cancer. I was skeptical of Trudeau's chances.

Brazeau was not your average senator. At thirty-four, he had become the youngest member of the Canadian Senate. He had held the position of national chief of the Congress of Aboriginal Peoples. He had served in the Naval Reserve. He was a second-degree black belt in karate. Second degree—as in murder. And a wrestler. Brazeau was favoured to win three to one. He was under a lot of pressure from Conservatives who wanted to see the Liberal Party's poster boy publicly humiliated.

The senator might have been the only person in the country cockier than Justin Trudeau. At the weigh-in, when the ref mentioned Justin's longer reach, Brazeau shoved his hand into his bikini briefs and said, "Whoa! I've got a lot of length over here." I had to cover that fight.

I asked Justin to spar with me ahead of the match. I mean, who hadn't dreamt of one day punching Justin Trudeau in the face? We met up at the gym he trained at in Montreal. Justin sparred with his trainer while I took some cheap shots. I asked him if his parents put him in boxing lessons so that Joe Clark's daughter would stop beating him up. "That's just not fair," he said. "She's got a mean left hook."

Justin told me that he didn't want to actually hit me when we boxed. "I don't want to hurt you," he said, hurting my ego. The piece wouldn't work if we were just shadowboxing, though. I'd have to make him want to hit me. "It's not like on the playground when somebody hits you," I said, needling him. "You can't say, 'My daddy's the prime minister! Leave me alone!' and lick your giant lollipop."

I saw him bristle for the second time. Clearly, his upbringing was a sore point.

"Okay, you're getting to me now, Critch," he said, with half a smile. He knew what my game was, but he also knew that it was working. "You think that's how my dad raised me?" he asked, firing off another combination.

"No. I know. That's not the way at all," I answered. Then I leaned in, nice and close, and called him "Trudy."

"Get your stuff on," he said. "We're gonna go."

I changed into boxing shorts, gloves and a shiny red robe with "Cocky" written on the back. The bell rang and he immediately punched me in the face. Stunned, I blocked his next punch, opening my torso up so he quickly punched me in the stomach. Then he hit me there a second time, then my chin again. He did not let up. He put one hand behind his back to humiliate me further. I knew I was no Jack Dempsey but I was surprised at just how fast he was.

Once the shoot was over, we sat in a corner of the gym chatting. I asked him if he was worried about getting hurt in the match with Brazeau. If it went as poorly as people were expecting, then it could also have a real effect on his political career, making him even more of a joke than he already was in some circles.

"There's something you should know about me," he told me. "People have been underestimating me my whole life. I don't start things unless I'm absolutely sure that I can win them."

Oh, I thought. *He's an egomaniac.*

I made sure that I was there on fight night. The room was electric. It was like a cross between election night and a cockfight. Conservative MPs filled the room. They were hopped up like kids on Christmas morning. Justin entered the ring gently bobbing his head to the music. The bell rang and Brazeau wasted no time in ringing Justin's bell. He pounded away at the taller fighter, like a lumberjack leaning into a redwood with his axe. Justin's legs turned to rubber and I thought for sure that he was going down. He kept standing throughout the first round through sheer stubbornness.

Trudeau came out strong in the second round, pushing Brazeau to the ropes with a series of ten straight jabs. It was Brazeau's turn to feel his legs turn to jelly. He had emptied his tank in the first round and then he found himself on a long stretch of highway without a gas station for miles. By the third round, Brazeau was having as much trouble breathing as I do when the escalator breaks in a mall. Trudeau forced his opponent into a corner and began to pummel him. I jumped up on my chair for a better view. It was unlike anything I had ever seen. It took two politicians in a charity match to get me into sports.

I caught up with Justin right after the fight. I couldn't help but think of the overconfident senator waving his junk around at the weigh-in. "Well," I said, "he's not swinging his pickle around now, is he? You were unbearable before," I told him. "I can't imagine what you're going to be like now. Pretty soon you'll be talking about yourself in the fourth person."

After the fight, people's opinions about Trudeau slowly began to change. He surprised no one when he announced a run for the Liberal leadership. In one skit, I wrapped him up in bubble wrap and put a helmet on him for protection. After all, he was the party's only hope. Justin played along as he always did. Whenever we needed a bit for the show, he was happy to oblige. But that all changed once he became leader.

~

The Liberals had been floating the idea of legalizing pot, and I was getting worried that the Canadian government would somehow find a way to take the fun out of weed. I wasn't sure about a world where calling your dealer meant hearing, "Hello, *bienvenu*, Cannabis Canada. For service in English, press 1. *Pour le service en français, appuyez sur le 2.*"

I thought, if anything, weed should be sold right where Canadians were used to buying their drug of choice: Tim Hortons. You'd just pull into the drive-thru and say, "Give me a Jamaican bacon breakfast sandwich served with hash browns made with real hash."

Trudeau made headlines when he admitted that he had smoked pot while an MP. I arranged an interview in his office and when the cameras were rolling I produced a joint from my pocket. "Where can I light up around here?" I asked.

"You're kidding," he said as I popped the joint in my mouth. "You didn't bring that into Parliament! You're not gonna hotbox my office! No way," he said, and pulled the lighter from my hand. For the first time since I'd known him, he ran completely cold. The staff in his office did too, and when the shoot was over, my cameraman Pete and I packed up our gear in silence. I couldn't understand the reaction because I didn't think I had done anything wrong.

Later that same day, I saw Justin in the foyer of the House of Commons. I shouted a word of thanks but, as I passed, he grabbed my hand and pulled me in close to him. "You're in trouble," he said. Thinking he was joking, I laughed in his face. He bristled for the third time and turned back to the legitimate press while I turned to Pete, a member of the illegitimate press.

"Does he seem pissed off to you?" I asked him.

"Who cares?" Pete said. "Let's get a beer." Pete always gave good advice. We went for a beer and I thought no more of it until later that night when we returned to our hotel, the Château Laurier. Trudeau's communications director, Kate Purchase, was waiting outside with a request from "the leader."

It took me a moment to realize who she was talking about, as I'd never heard him referred to as that. "You mean Justin?"

Kate asked me not to use the joint clip. Trudeau was trying to get away from the pot-smoking image and did not want a video of himself with a joint out there. I thought the whole situation was laughable, even for a comedian.

I told her that it was a little late to put this particular genie back in the bong. Trudeau was as much a natural pairing to pot as papers were.

But she stood firm. If the clip aired we might not get access to Trudeau anymore.

I didn't like politicians—or their staff—telling me what I could and could not air. Kate was Trudeau's communications director. I was not.

The piece aired and it quickly went viral. When later asked about it by Canada.com, Kate confirmed that she'd asked for a portion of the segment to be cut "as it was a highly inappropriate thing to do in a parliamentary office."

Justin Trudeau ran to become prime minister in 2015. The Liberals turned down our request for an interview, but as luck would have it, our paths would cross, whether Justin wanted them to or not.

Producer Cory and cameraman Pete were already on the road covering the election, and I was joining them to interview Conservative MP Chris Alexander. Alexander was all over the news because of a press conference in which he and MP Kellie Leitch announced Harper's disastrous snitch line for "barbaric cultural practices." His career was so far in the toilet that he agreed to try on Halloween costumes with me. My plan was to scare him with the most frightening thing he could imagine—a hijab.

I landed in Toronto with a bag full of costumes, wigs and beards. Cory texted, "Trudeau's bus is here. Come right away." I grabbed my bag and rushed to their motel just in time to see Justin's bus, emblazoned with his smiling face, pulling out of the parking lot. I tossed my stuff into the back seat, Cory and Pete jumped in, and we gave chase.

We pulled in behind the bus and ran into the supermarket where Trudeau was speaking and tucked in behind the rest of the media, without a plan. We were setting up the shot when I felt a hand on my shoulder. It was Gerald Butts, the architect behind Trudeau's platform, his future principal secretary and the man who would one day fall on his sword for Justin during the SNC-Lavalin scandal. Hoping to avoid a scene in front of the press, Gerry told me that it just so happened that Justin would have some time for me after all. Gerry was a Cape Bretoner, so I trusted him. "And don't worry," I told him, "I didn't bring any pot."

But what to do with Trudeau now that I had him? I stared down at my bag of Halloween costumes. Trudeau was trying to entice millennials to vote for the first time. *I know,* I thought. *I'll ask him what advice he would have had for himself when he was younger.* And I would do that dressed as his younger self.

I reached into my bag and pulled on a shaggy wig. I taped a moustache and goatee onto my face and undid the buttons on my shirt. I made my best attempt at emulating Justin's early *Puss in Boots* years. Back then, with shaggy hair and a goatee, he looked less like an MP and more like a background dancer in a touring production of *The Pirates of Penzance.*

"Hey, Justin," I said in a surfer dude voice. "It's me. You from 2011."

"Oh dear," he said, finally relaxing a little and playing along. "This is the federal election campaign. It's 2015."

"Great," I enthused. "How's Prime Minister Ignatieff?" I asked my "future self" what advice he had for me/him.

"You need to button up that shirt," he told me, "you need to get a haircut, you need to shave and you need to work really, really hard."

"Oh my god," I said. "Work hard? Get a haircut? Shave? I'm a Conservative?"

And with that, we were fine again. We chatted while Pete packed up his camera gear and I asked him if he really thought he had a chance at winning this thing.

"Remember when we boxed," he said, "and I told you I don't start something unless I am completely sure that I can win it? Don't underestimate me. I'm going to win."

I was there at Montreal's Queen Elizabeth Hotel when he did just that and became Canada's twenty-third prime minister. I stood in the back of the room and shook my head. I couldn't believe that I was watching the same guy I had brushed off at another rally twelve years earlier. Twice I had underestimated him. Twice he had proved me wrong. I wouldn't make that mistake a third time.

Tensions between Trudeau and *22 Minutes* eased to the point where I travelled with him on the prime minister's plane. We went to

Washington to cover the state dinner President Obama threw for him. I walked through the Rose Garden and the Press Room reminiscing about my trip to the basement. I felt a tap on my shoulder and a voice shouted, "What are you doing here?" I turned to see the same man who had snuck me into the basement years before. This time, I wasn't worried about getting kicked out.

I asked Trudeau about his bromance with Obama and begged him to look at me the way he'd looked at the president. We gazed into each other's eyes as Dan Hill's "Sometimes When We Touch" played. Then he asked me, "Do we get to kiss now?"

I couldn't imagine Harper doing that.

~

On a bright summer's day in 2016, Justin Trudeau made a visit to my hometown of St. John's, Newfoundland and Labrador. I took my kids up to Signal Hill so they could see the PM in person and maybe hear him speak. That wasn't an opportunity they'd had when Stephen Harper visited in 2015. He spoke at an invite-only event for one hundred people in a cold storage facility. I guess they didn't want him to melt.

My sons and I were climbing up the winding road to Cabot Tower to see Harper's successor. On the way there, the boys asked me, "You're not going to embarrass us, are you?"

I was shocked. I thought I was pretty cool. "What do you mean?" I asked.

"I don't know," Jacob said worriedly. "I mean, you're not gonna do some goofy stunt, are you?"

I was heartbroken. I didn't always have to be the centre of attention. Yes, I was a comedian, but I wasn't a clown. I assured my sons that I would never do anything like that as I planned to do exactly that.

At the time, Trudeau was in the news for a series of photobombs. He had been spotted jogging behind some high school students as they took their grad photos by Vancouver's seawall. He was shirtless and holding a surfboard when he photobombed a beach wedding in

Tofino. A family was hiking in Quebec's Gatineau Park when a shirtless Trudeau emerged from the woods for a photo. At this point Shirtless Trudeau sightings were as legendary as Bigfoot sightings.

I introduced the PM to my sons, and Justin was very kind. Then, as he was walking away, I couldn't help myself. "Hang on a second," I said, putting my hand on the prime minister's arm and gently guiding him to stand in front of me, facing away.

He looked confused but not surprised. "What are you going to do?"

"Just keep looking forward," I said behind him as I took off my shirt to the sound of a hundred camera clicks. Justin turned around just as I was covering my pale, translucent skin with my shirt again. I turned to my boys. "See what happens when you ask me not to embarrass you?" If they could have rolled their eyes any further into their skulls they would have been permanently blinded.

The picture immediately went viral like nothing I had ever done before. #shirtlessCritch was trending on Twitter. Thousands of people retweeted the picture of what looked like our prime minister standing next to a bag of white milk in jeans. Trudeau is standing with his arms out, unaware of what is happening behind him. Spectators and security alike are all laughing, and MP Seamus O'Regan is covering his mouth and giggling like a little kid. It's just a silly, joyful photograph that connected with people. The story was picked up by everyone from *Entertainment Tonight* to Buzzfeed.

People kept asking me when the full skit was going to air on *22 Minutes*. "There isn't one," I told them. "I wasn't trying to shoot a skit. I was just trying to embarrass my kids." I had become the living embodiment of a dad joke—a dad-bod joke.

Trudeau was riding high in the polls. He showed up on the cover of *Rolling Stone*. Marvel put him on the cover of a comic book. The only thing that could stop him was him. And right on cue, in January of 2017, Trudeau got himself into hot water yet again, just by swimming in it. He accepted a family vacation on the private Bahamian island of the Aga Khan, the leader of the world's Ismaili Muslims. The Aga

Khan is also chairman of the board of the Global Centre for Plural-ism, an institution to which the federal government had pledged a $15-million grant. There was, perhaps, a small conflict of interest.

To try to change the topic, Trudeau started criss-crossing the coun-try giving a series of town halls. Between private islands and speaking tours, I was wondering if he was ever going to make it back to Ottawa again. Pete, Cory and I caught up with him at the town hall in Halifax. The prime minister gave us some one-on-one time before the event. I was starting to worry that our interviews were becoming too buddy-buddy. Trudeau had, except when a joint was pulled in his office, always been eager to play along. I decided to go for broke and see if I couldn't upset the apple cart a little.

I brought along a cat collar with a little bell on it. I told him I was going to put it on him so Canadians would be able to find him the next time he wandered off somewhere like an island.

I don't know if you've ever tried to put a cat's collar on a sitting prime minister. I wouldn't recommend it. Trudeau's eyes flashed at me and then at the collar and then back up to my face. "You're not putting that on me," he said with half a laugh.

"Oh yes I am," I said, and reached for his neck. Trudeau blocked me, but I squirmed my arms loose and tried to wrap the collar around his neck.

"This is not happening," he said, the giggle now long gone from his voice.

Over the years I had gotten pretty comfortable around Justin Trudeau. I had covered him in bubble wrap, I had boxed him, I had combed his moustache and I had wrestled him for a joint. In that moment in Halifax, he ceased to be the prime minister to me. He was just a guy who was being a bit of a baby and wouldn't put on a cat's collar. The more he tried to stop me, the more determined I was to get that thing around his neck.

I caught Cory's face out of the corner of my eye. His mouth was open. He gently shook his head. I saw Pete, next to him. His head was cocked and he was no longer looking in his viewfinder. The Mounties on Trudeau's detail did not look pleased that I was desperately trying to get my hands around the prime minister's throat.

I snapped back to my senses, pulled away from him and lowered the collar. "Thanks so much for doing this," I said, winding up the interview. The room would have been completely silent were it not for the jingle-jangle of the cat bell in my hand.

"What the hell was that?" Pete asked as we drove home.

"I don't think that . . . worked," Cory added diplomatically.

Comedy is not an exact science. Sometimes I made mistakes. Not as many as Trudeau. But I did make mistakes. It doesn't matter if you know the person who is in the prime minister's seat or not. You still have to show respect for the office, no matter who it is. I wasn't talking to the mop-headed MP for Papineau anymore. I was talking to the prime minister.

~

The week before the 2020 US election, which was also in the middle of the COVID-19 pandemic, I interviewed Trudeau. I tried to get him to comment on the dumpster fire next door. "Your father once compared living next to the USA to sleeping with an elephant. But now the elephant is awake, he's up all night tweeting from the toilet and he's high on steroids. Is America still an elephant or is it more like a *Tyrannosaurus rex* with two handguns?"

Trudeau danced around without managing to say much of anything about Trump at all.

That didn't surprise me. By then, he had managed to survive the WE Charity scandal; an ill-fated trip to India in which he dressed like it was the official state visit of Mr. Dressup; ethics violations; and the SNC-Lavalin scandal in which the ethics commissioner found Trudeau had attempted to "circumvent, undermine and ultimately attempt to discredit" Canada's first Indigenous female attorney general and justice minister, not to mention blackface and brownface. Maybe a pandemic didn't seem all that bad in comparison.

I have known the man for a long time now. I'm not a close friend, but I've watched him enough to know two truths about him:

1. He is his own worst enemy.
2. He is not to be underestimated.

~

When I was starting out, I would have to lie, sneak and risk arrest to get an interview with a prime minister. Now, I just have to ask. The first prime minister I ever interviewed was forty-one years my senior. The current one is just three years older than me, but at least he's still older. If I'm lucky, there may soon come a day when I interview one who is younger than I am.

When I look back, the road from Chrétien to Trudeau seems both infinitely long and uncomfortably short. It's a road I am still on, and I am as curious to find out where it leads today as I was when I started walking it.

When I was seventeen my father asked me what I wanted to be when I grew up. I hope to God that I never find out.

HOME AGAIN

F ISH HAVE A WAY of finding their way back home. This behaviour is best exemplified by salmon. They can migrate out to the sea to feed for years on end but, one day, inexplicably, something pulls them home. Somehow they find their way back to the same stream, and sometimes even the very same part of the stream, where they were born.

Some scientists theorize they might be following the pattern of the earth's magnetic field. Others think that they might be particularly sensitive to the unique chemical odours of the streams they hatched in. But no one really knows. I don't either. But I do know the feeling.

In 2012, I was cast in a film called *The Grand Seduction* alongside beloved Irish actor Brendan Gleeson of *Braveheart* and *Harry Potter* fame and my old pal and Canadian icon Gordon Pinsent. The film is set in Newfoundland and Labrador. In it, residents of a small fishing community charm a doctor into becoming the town's full-time physician in order to secure a vital factory contract. The film was shot in the area around my beloved Trinity. So once more, twenty years after I had left the town in search of brighter lights, I found myself spending the summer acting in Trinity.

My love for Trinity had never faltered over the years and the miles. Trinity had lost none of its timelessness, either. One of the blacksmiths was still firing up his forge. The lighthouse still moaned its warning, and Donna Butt's actors still filled the streets for the Trinity Pageant.

But I was not the only thing about Trinity that had changed in the intervening years.

Donna's actors no longer had to perform outside in fields or in the parish hall. Donna had managed to raise $1 million to build a proper theatre. The 250-seat complex hugged the cliffs of Green's Point where we had once performed *A Midsummer Night's Dream*. It stood on the footprint of the fishing premises that had stood there for three hundred years.

The merchant families who owned those fishing rooms once exported the area's wealth to England. Now, for once, the people who lived there were reaping the benefits. Restaurants and B&Bs were flourishing. A brewery had opened. And now a movie was being filmed there. The place felt alive, and the locals were working. The more I walked the familiar paths, the more I felt at peace.

It was practically impossible to be glum in the company of my co-stars. One day, as we waited for a camera set-up near the tiny community of Tickle Cove (population thirty), Gordon asked me if I wanted to wander over to the little roadside store. Gordon's childhood nickname was Porky and for good reason. He never met a snack he didn't like.

The bell above the door cheerfully announced us as we entered the tiny shop. The shelves were filled as much with dust as they were with groceries. The little old lady behind the counter looked up in disbelief as she found herself in the presence of the great Gordon Pinsent. She motioned for me to come over.

"Young man," she asked, "do you work for Mr. Pinsent?"

"My love," I answered, "don't we all?"

"Would I be able to meet him, do you think?"

"Well," I whispered over the counter, "seeing as he is about to buy a bag of chips and you're the only one on cash, it seems to me to be a certainty."

"Oh my," she said, straightening her shirt and adjusting her hair. "And me without my makeup."

I wandered over to the Codfather and leaned into his ear. "You got a fan, here, Gordo. Lay it on thick, will ya?"

Gordon selected a package of potato chips and made a beeline for the counter. "Madame," he said, taking her hand, "may I say that this is one of the finest establishments I have ever had the privilege of shopping in. Are you the daughter of the owners?"

"Oh, no, Mr. Pinsent," she said, giggling. "I *am* the owner. Oh my lord." Sixty years fell from her face in an instant as Gordon gently kissed her wrist. He then bid her good day, spun on his heels and left the store.

The bell above the door announced his departure, and I smiled at the proprietor as I, too, made my way out of the lonely shop.

"Excuse me," she called out, the years returning to her face. "You owe me two bucks for his chips." Ah, to be famous.

Brendan, Gordon and I would sit between takes and talk about acting, music and love. I once asked Gordon what his favourite time of day was.

"You know that time in the morning," he told me, "when you're not yet quite awake? It only lasts a moment but part of you is still dreaming. I often reach for my Charm then," he said, mentioning his late wife. "In that moment it seems she is still there with me. That's the best part of my day."

I had never heard such a perfect description of all-encompassing love before, and I silently wondered if I would ever find someone to miss that much. And then I did.

~

I saw a St. John's lawyer named Melissa Royle being interviewed on the CTV morning chat show *Canada AM*. A picture of her swimming in the ocean next to an iceberg had gone viral. The show's host Jeff Hutcheson described her as a "nutcase." How could you not love that?

We started dating. She knew more about politics and Newfoundland history than I did, and I hung on her every word.

I asked her one day if she had ever been to Trinity. She had not. We threw some clothes in a bag and hopped into the car. Three hours later, we crested the top of the same hill I had first seen in 1993.

"Do I turn right or left?" Melissa asked.

"It doesn't matter," I told her. "It's a loop. Lady's choice." Melissa turned to the right, and I noticed someone had just tapped a For Sale sign on a little house tucked in beneath a cliff right on the water's edge. It had been a one-room grocery store in the nearby community of Plate Cove, and when the store closed, someone thought it a shame to waste such a sturdy spot and dragged it over to Trinity.

"I know this sounds crazy," I told her, "but I think I'm going to buy that house." And before the weekend was over, I did.

Melissa and I got married in Trinity on August 3, 2018, in the oldest wooden church in Newfoundland.

Even though I had returned to Trinity, the cod that left in 1993 still had not yet come back. At least not in the numbers that would have allowed the fishery to open back up to its past glory. However, each year there is a recreational food fishery, where people are allowed to catch five fish each—fifteen cod maximum per boat—and our wedding just so happened to fall on one of those days.

The night before the wedding, my friend Jeremy Charles asked me what I wanted to do before I got married. I told him that there was only one thing to do—catch a fish.

Jeremy is the co-owner and head chef of Raymonds Restaurant in St. John's—one of the very best restaurants in the country. He is also an excellent fisherman. "I'll meet you at the wharf, six thirty tomorrow morning," he told me.

My friend of thirty years Harry Bartlett was waiting by the wharf in his boat then, too. His partner, Tina Randell, was one of the first people I'd met when I first came to Trinity. It was good to see the friendship had lasted.

The sunlight danced on the waves of the Atlantic Ocean as we felt the once common tug on the end of our lines. I dropped my handline over the side of the boat and caught my five within minutes. Other boats bobbed on the water around us as the sea came to life with fishers once more. It was as if the ocean had been sleeping and now it, too, had remembered what it was like in the old days. When the folks in the other boats heard that we were hoping to get some fish for the wedding, they offered us their catches. It was the miracle of the loaves and fishes all over again. We cleaned the fish on the wharf and then I rushed to clean off the fish guts and get dressed for the wedding.

As we stood at the altar, the priest asked us to turn around to face the crowd. "Give yourselves a moment to take it in," he told us. "These are the people in your life and they are here because they love you." My eyes scanned the room. The *22 Minutes* cast, Cory and Pete, Gordon, Tristy, and my boys—they were all there. Many of my friends from those early days were there, too. The whole thing seemed like it could have been a scene in the Trinity Pageant, and I couldn't have been happier for my role.

Donna let us have our reception in her new theatre. I could not have felt more at home had it been in my house. We bought out the Dinner Theatre and, instead of a show, we had music from our talented friends. Alan Doyle led a who's who of Newfoundland and Labrador's finest. People often use the phrase "we danced all night," but that night we truly did.

My boys welcomed Melissa into the family in a traditionally sarcastic Critch manner. "We're so glad that Dad found Melissa," Jacob said, "because now we don't have to pay to put him in a home." The boys got the biggest laughs in a room full of comedians. I could not have been prouder.

That night, while everyone danced, Jeremy worked away out on the wharf. He filled a giant pot with fish that could only be fresher if they were still swimming. He served it up as a late-night snack. I stood on the wharf, staring up at the Trinity stars, eating the most satisfying meal of my life. I had never been so sure that I had landed in the right place.

Everything had come full circle for me in that moment. The end of the fishery had brought me to Trinity, where I had been a fish out of water. My career had taken me all over the world, but as it turned out, I needn't have gone much farther than Trinity to find my place in it. Trinity had once seemed the farthest place in the world from home to me. But now, having cast my net, and caught my limit, I was finally home.

NOTES

PROLOGUE

the most famous joke in the world was born a stone's throw from my house Ann Anderson, *Snake Oil, Hustlers and Hambones: The American Medicine Show*, McFarland Publishing, 2004.

"headaches, earaches, toothaches, neuralgia, cuts, scalds, sprains, rheumatic aches and pains" Thomas P. Kelley, "My Dad Was King of the Medicine Men," *Maclean's*, March 14, 1959.

ACKNOWLEDGMENTS

I stumble wildly through life and am only kept from falling on my face by the caring people who catch me and right me. I have a lot of people to thank.

At Penguin Random House Canada, I would be lost without the leadership of Nicole Winstanley and Scott Sellers. Thanks to Beth Cockeram for her marketing genius and to my incredible publicist Dan French. Leah Springate and Terri Nimmo provided the lovely design and the cover that you probably judged this book by. And a huge thanks to my editor, Laura Dosky, for her guidance, patience and gentle nudging.

Thanks to my former literary agent, Madeline Wilson, for getting me to sea and my current agent, Michael Levine, and the team at Westwood Creative Artists for seeing me safely to shore.

I have to thank my sons, Jacob and Will, for their constant support and for making my heart burst with pride. Thank you to my brother Mike for always having my back and my soul brother Tristy Clark for being the best friend I could ever hope for.

Thank you to my wife, Melissa, for being the smartest person I know. I am delighted to be the worst decision you ever made. And to Cathie, Dave, Mike, Jess and Pop, thanks for dinner conversation that is much cheaper than therapy.

And, of course, a huge thanks to my *22 Minutes* family. In my years there, there have been too many people to mention, but thank you for taking a chance on me and for letting me come play. To Tracey Jardine, thank you for all of your help. Special thanks to Cory, Pete, Tim, Mike and Peter for the lifelong friendships, honesty and lies.

And to Donna Butt and the people of Trinity, thanks for giving me my start and for taking a prodigal son back home.